To: Ron
Conten
we need you!
Pennie

Giving Myself Permission!

The simplest path to successful living

Pennie Murray

LX Unlimited Publishing
Kansas City, Mo.

Giving Myself Permission!

Scripture References are the author's paraphrases from the Life Application Bible.

ISBN: 0-9651942-1-3

Library of Congress 2002091235

Published by:
LX Unlimited · *P.O. Box 893 · Grandview, Mo · 64030*
(816) 965-5823

Giving Myself Permission!

Pennie Murray

To My Children, Ilyce & LeAlec

Who have been courageous and forgiving enough to allow me to grow-up and love me through my journey of finding the power of Giving Myself Permission.

God could not have given me better.
I Love You!

I dedicate this book to my four sisters:

Iris, Arzella, Sheila & Bridgett
Who like me, in their own very different ways have struggled with giving themselves permission to live and breath in the power of their intended purpose and unique identity.

May the internal wisdom and love of God overtake you!

Contents

First Impression 6

Personal Note 8

Permission, a Word of Power 10

Professional Sleepwalkers 18

The Issue Is Not that We Are Weak 32

Success Is a Tapestry 53

What's the Shortest Distance? 69

The Afterglow 91

First Impression

As I prepared mentally for the undertaking of this book, I began to envision the different personalities you find in a bookstore. My mind lingered on the shopper who would see a book entitled, "Giving Myself Permission" and think, "What do you mean, giving myself permission? That's ludicrous, of course I have permission, I'm grown, I'm an adult."

Just in case you know one of those people or you are that person who has given yourself permission to go beyond the cover of this book, here is a question for you:

Do you know the direct, indirect and lingering impact this thing called *PERMISSION* can have on the events, circumstances and direction of your life?

For instance, during a performance review, you failed to seize the opportunity to negotiate a higher salary for yourself because you feared what your boss would think of you, or you were afraid to challenge the status quo.

Have you ever wanted to say NO, but out of guilt or baseless obligation, you said YES? Have you ever tried to set boundaries with your job, family, loved ones or friends—to get others to respect your time and space, without being overwhelmed with feelings of selfishness and betrayal? Do you believe that stress and crisis management at home and at work is the price you pay for success? Do you believe that relaxation is a passive act of nothingness strictly for those with nothing to do? Is your emotional relationship with God, family, spouse, significant other and friends filled with paranoia, defensiveness and lack of trust?

All of these and many, many more life events and issues are strongly dictated and affected by how and from whom we feel we must receive our permission to live.

Giving oneself permission suggests that we leave behind the crutches and cushions of our life and become self-directed and purposeful. It suggests a moving forward toward a continued life-style of excellence that upsets the mindset of average thinking.

Now, if you're satisfied with your present conditions and circumstances of life and you desire no more than what you already have, who am I to suggest that you challenge the comfortable? But if, just if, the thought of there possibly being more for you, that in the marrow of your imagination there is a suspicion of greatness, then you are ready to come out and play amongst the legends.

"Giving Myself Permission" is not for the faint of heart. Its mission is to stretch you beyond the familiar and to give you the fuel to challenge your status quo and change your present limited conditions. It is a guidebook to understanding that the "*power of permission*" is authorized by you—not granted by others.

A Personal Note:

As an instructor of personal success education, I have facilitated many in group coaching sessions, seminars and workshops on the elements that sabotage and hinder the desired success of the two most important areas of anyone's life—professional career and personal relationships.

I have wept with countless participants as they shared their hidden desires and abandoned dreams with tears of anguish and a sense of guilt. They spoke of an unsettled yearning, a haunting of incompleteness that brought them to that particular session in quest of instruction and discovery. A haunting and yearning that many of us are all too familiar with when life is not lived in its greatest form of authenticity.

Even though the unanimous intended desire of any one of those groups was of personal success, repeatedly I would experience overwhelming unconscious resistance from at least a quarter of the attendees. A resistance that ranged from total and complete denial to the use of elaborate, well rehearsed excuses of "can't, because…"

These episodes would leave me exhausted, baffled and concerned. What was I not seeing? Was there a bridging factor, another piece that kept them comfortable in their state of paralysis? Why couldn't they "just do it?"

Then it hit me—the missing piece, a very important piece called "*PERMISSION*," the act of approving or granting consent for a particular course of action. Permitting ourselves to receive the restoration of a broken marriage, to have confidence in our abilities and resourcefulness, to accept an unconditional love from an unconditional God, to know that we are worthy of a good love and a good life, to accept that we are healed of our emotional or physical injuries and to completely love ourselves.

In this book we will look at the action of permission, how it relates to our successes and the effects it has on even the simplest areas of our lives. It is my hope that this book will allow you to see that the only permission you need now—or ever—is your own.

So if you are as excited as I am and ready to release the flow of your internal abundance and bring forth a successful living experience, let's get your life flames going again.

I only request two things as we move forward. First, that you keep in mind our goal in the beginning of this process is only to obtain a five percent heightened level of internal trust in you, God and your purpose. Second, that you embrace the fact that anything, everything is possible within you from this moment on.

Pennie

1

Permission, a Word of Power

"When you take charge of your life, there is no longer a need to ask permission to be. When you ask permission from other people or society, at large, you give them veto power over you and your life.

—Geoffery F. Abert

I remember playing a childhood game called "Mother may I?" The general idea of the game was to reach the finish line by getting permission before making any advancing moves. If you moved without remembering to ask "Mother may I?" you were to go back to your starting point. And of course the one who was able to comply quickly and remember to ask permission every time would win. Given there was no favoritism involved.

So a number of us would line up at a designated starting point excitedly awaiting acknowledgement and instructions on how many steps each would be permitted to take. Did we forget to ask permission? You bet! Were we sent back? Yep.

After a few times of being sent back the excitement and motivation would began to dwindle. I would see one kid just standing idle with her thumb in her mouth, expecting a "no win." Another would be ranting and screaming, "Cheat, that's no fair!"

Instead of high energy and boastful certainty, the mood would change to "Who cares about winning? This is a dumb game anyway." And the group would begin to disperse one by one—maybe it was our lost spirit to win, our perceived biasness, unrealistic expectations, an inability to conform, or just plain old fashion boredom. Whatever the reason, the fire and passion to win were replaced with melancholy. Some, slowly, aimlessly looked for another activity or someone else to play with. Others made a beeline to their bikes and created their own enjoyment. While still others stood shouting, stomping and fanning their arms, "Come back here, the game's not over! Come back, you can't do that, we're not through playing!"

It's amazing how a simple game like this and other subtle life learnings have caused some to cling tightly to self-direction and accelerate through life with complete focus, determination and assuredness. Others wander, frustrated and dejected, waiting for someone, anyone to give them permission to go, to do and to be, and still others remain stuck in anger, demanding what they feel entitled to.

What was it in those children, the ones who wasted no time in redirecting themselves and creating their own enjoyment? What did they possess internally that allowed them to maintain their self-commitment, their ability to re-channel their vitality and intensity of expression?

I am convinced that they knew and honored the power of "self-permission." They gave themselves permission to not win every game—to walk away without pity or anger—and they knew life as optional, not compulsory or automatic. They gave themselves permission to make choices that were not dependent on the approving attitudes, opinions and behavior of others.

Bill Cosby once said, "I don't know the key to success, but the key to failure is trying to please everybody." The action of self-permission opens us up to our enterprising self, a self that has absolutely nothing to do with external effects. It is a force of energy able to exert knowledge, authority and influence anywhere, at anytime.

Those who exercise their power of self-permission daily are often unaware of its existence, because for them it has always been a part of their character. They marvel and shake their heads at the thought of others not being able to do the same.

For those who are adequately skilled in the power of self-permission, this book can assist in checking the quality and content of your use of self-permission. For those of us who thought we were skilled in self-permission and those who are not, this book will assist in laying the proper groundwork to begin to recognize, develop and use this energy effectively.

We are all born with a nature of desire, purpose and determination. We long to be self-confident, when in reality our desire is to be self-possessing, to have full autonomy of our intrinsic abilities, feelings and behavior. To have our individualism respected and celebrated, not judged and condemned. It is for the sake of these internal longings that we consider the value and meaning life can have through self-permission.

The word *PERMISSION* is a word of action, an exercise of the Mind and Will. Exercising the *Will* deliberately chooses and decides on a course of action. The *Will* possess the natural gifts of discipline, diligence, determination and purpose. While the *Will* does play a major role in self-permission, the *Mind* has a greater effect and influence on action. With "Permission" being an action word and the *Mind* having a greater influence on action, then the goal here would be to somehow change the *Mind*.

Attempting to *change* someone's mind would be a good approach if I had nothing else to do, but it is not my goal to change anything, so we can all relax. Because the mind has the inherent ability to think, to reason and then to apply knowledge, my aim is to simply introduce another view for the sole purpose of challenging and stimulating the "mind" to do what it does best.

I have incredible faith in the human soul, which consist of the mind, will and emotions. I believe that if the soul is provided with the what's and why's of life, it will find its own way. Our conscious mind responds to information and events based on the stimulation it receives from our perceptions, emotions, memory and imagination. Our initial resistance to new information is usually the result of our misperceptions or our emotional restrictions. In order to relieve some of the internal opposition, we will need to eliminate what self-permission is not.

Self-permission is not the same as "willpower." Willpower is the mental ability to deliberately choose to carry out one's decisions, wishes or plans. Self-permission, on the other hand, grants the action of carrying out a decision, wish or plan. Using willpower without self-permission causes the mind to perceive our actions as domination, denial or restriction. The mind then becomes resentful and will either rebel, shut down or undermine our efforts.

Self-permission is not "selfish." Selfishness is the obsessive preoccupation of self that excludes us from appreciating or respecting others. Selfishness has a character of superficiality, unnecessary pessimism, self-preservation, wait-and-see attitude and self-pity, to name just a few. Self-permission merely allows, lets happen and offers possibilities. It has a character of empowerment, declaration of faith and authentication. It is unconditional, patient and tolerant. However, if not properly developed, self-permission will allow selfishness to emerge instead of our qualities of excellence.

Cycle of Self-Permission

When I began in corporate training, I believed the needs were in the areas of efficacy, technical and competency skills. However, over the years, participants began to reveal deeper distresses. Anxieties of feeling incompetent, unfulfilled, insignificant, lacking assertiveness and feeling imprisoned within their own lives.

When I began to integrate what I call personal success education into my training techniques, Pandora's box opened. The more personal interaction I had with participates, the more I faced the glaring question: "Why?" Why was this intelligent, very competent and able person not experiencing a greater level of fulfillment? Then the question turn inwardly and it became imperative that the answer be found.

It's not that we are incompetent. We just never give ourselves permission to allow true virtue to surface. Through guilt and mental conditioning, we have learned to always color inside the lines and to never look outside the box. Our mental predisposition tells us that only the elite (whoever they are) taste the sweet nectar of success. Whenever we feel unfulfilled, it's because we are staying true to our programmed limits and we remain in less challenging positions and situations in order to appease the voices of restriction. Stretching ourselves beyond what comes easy for us leaves us awkward and not in control. Giving ourselves permission would move us out of our comfort zone, beyond the voices of limit, to the temporary unknown for greater growth and opportunity.

In order to experience self-permission, a mental readiness is required. A preparedness that will help us find personal worthiness enough to give ourselves permission and to live above and beyond average. The "Cycle of Permission" is a process of maturity, a development that starts with the *acknowledgment* of a desire, *accepting* our personal worthiness to have that desire, a willingness to *ask* for what is desired and to have a sense of *anticipation* for what is asked and lastly to give *permission* to receive the results of the asking. The cycle is one of acknowledgement, acceptance, asking, anticipating and permitting.

Acknowledgement moves us to recognize a want; it admits to the existence of our desire as reality and truth. Acceptance strengthens our self-trust because we regard the desire as true and our belief validates it. Asking breeds confidence. Anticipation involves more than expecting—it is having a foretaste of something expected before it occurs or is even articulated. And permitting puts us in an open position of receiving.

However, if we lack a mental readiness, the cycle may begin, but it rarely goes full-circle because somewhere between asking and expecting, doubt moves in. Doubt that is largely due to our thoughts of whether or not we are deserving of it, whether our past attitudes and actions warrant receiving anything better.

What if we were to examine the effects an unforgiven internal self has on the external self, and what it permits to come into existence? What would we find? It is my belief that until there is complete reconciliation with the internal self, our external efforts will always be exhaustive and our outcomes always second best.

While our society embraces the need for reconciliation with others, there is little concern or discussion to reestablish a close relationship between our internal selves. To engage in reconciliation that would settle or resolve the brokenness, the judging, the resentment and the faultfinding between our spirit, our soul (mind, will, emotion) and our body. A reconciliation that would permit us to honor and regard ourselves with respect and appreciation, instead of the daily self-contempt and reproach many of us often indulge in.

Playing Average

They say that life is merely a stage and we are simply actors playing a role. Okay, if that's true, than do we have a choice in what role we play, or through some whimsical happening, are we thrown into a role, only to be typecast for the rest of our lives? Personally, I choose to believe that we have a choice. A choice of playing the role of excellence, good, average, mediocre or inferior. Most of us straddle the fence on *AVERAGE*, implying sufficiency, yet lacking distinction. While we are capable of greatness, even excellence, we tend to play it safe so that we do not draw to much attention to ourselves, for fear of what more would be expected of us.

Average is okay, but consider this: Some of us have been the prey of emotional and mental robbery—and intimidation was the weapon to take away our power of self-permission. Still others have never learned the skills required to recognize or use their power of permission. Hence, we become victims or survivors in our own lives, never able to prosper and grow to our intended level of fulfillment.

We are familiar with the victim who endures harm, suffering and disadvantage at the hands of another. However, there are also the victims who suffer injury and loss because of their own voluntary undertaking. Although they are very capable and competent, experience has taught them the skill of playing less than or weak. This role has its benefits. First, by playing less than, we never have to really be responsible to make decisions or create resolve. Secondly, we can get the attention of others as they marvel over our ability to endure such great suffering from the bullies of life. Oh, how proudly we can wear our badges of martyrdom, keeping them polished and never letting others forget our great sacrifices.

The role of survivor is often a role played not by choice. We play it because we lack the skills or talents needed to show that we have the initiative and the willingness to undertake new projects or to perform greater roles. If opportunity and support is unavailable in our life, past or present, then our self-confidence, reliance and courage suffer the tragic condition of "character dwarfism."

Giving ourselves permission is simple, yet it calls for us to engage in a contest, a fight to bring our true purpose and intended destiny to the surface. Regaining our possession of self will not happen in a brief struggle. There will be battles that will take place over time and at different levels, but nonetheless repossession can occur. You may be saying, "I thought this was to be the simplest path to success." Not only is this the simplest, it is the only way to true, long-lasting success, but you must do your first work first.

I would have to say the greatest example of this first work comes from an episode of "Star Wars; Return of the Jedi." In one particular scene, Luke Skywalker wanted to return to his homeland to answer a call of distress. Knowing he was in fact the chosen one, his teacher, Yoda, also knew that there was a crouching enemy waiting for just the right moment to destroy him. Before allowing him to return, Yoda instructed him to complete one last challenge. His only instruction was to enter into a very dark and dismal cave to face whatever was to come.

Within moments, he found himself in a swash-buckling laser fight with his archenemy, Darth Vader. After an intense struggle, Luke was able to overpower him and win the battle by cutting off his enemy's head. As the head rolled away the mask opened to reveal the face of his enemy—to his astonishment, the face was his own.

My confidence in the ability of this book to summon you into action is great. Whether or not you begin your process immediately is of no concern. The fact that you have this book in your hand is evidence enough that you are ready for internal change. The focus of this book is to assist in leveling the battleground and revealing the possible areas of attack. Armed with insight and information, there will be assurance of a lifetime of successful wins. That's why this is the simplest path to success.

As I said earlier, the intent of this book is not to change anyone's mind, but simply to stimulate the mind to do what it does best—think, reason and then apply knowledge. Throughout this book, it is my intent to challenge our comfort zones and our tendency to play small for the sake of another's ego, to encourage a mindset of individualized success and to recognize the shortest distance to our intended path.

If however, this is more than you want to deal with, it's always better not to start at all than to start and turn back. On the other hand, if you are ready to live life and live it more abundantly let's begin with our first permissive power challenge.

Permissive Power Challenge

Throughout the day, whenever you think of it, challenge yourself to have 5% more faith and trust in yourself.

The *5% more* is not based on your mind's present value of your past actions, behaviors and results, which we often feel dictates our worthiness to deserve. It is merely based on the simple act of permitting yourself to say it, accept it and then allow it to take its natural course of action.

There is no time span as to how long to challenge you and there are no pre-determined results or events. I personally do not believe in rushing excellence or limiting the hand of God with our finite understanding of time and results. There is no rush or pressure—5% more faith and trust is all we want to gain at this time. We will discuss the 5% theory later.

2

Professional Sleepwalkers

If you love sleep, you will end in poverty. Stay awake, work with endurance and there will be plenty to eat!
—Proverbs 20:13

The action of writing this book came in a series of what many would refer to as "wake-up calls." However, this would not be entirely correct since the term "wake-up" would indicate that there was an immediate sense of consciousness. Unfortunately, that was not the case. What I experienced over a period of three years was what I now call "shake-ups," the constant nudging, agitations and disruptions we receive while content with sleepwalking through life.

The American Heritage Dictionary defines *SLEEPWALKING* as "the act of performing activities associated with wakefulness while in a sleeplike state." This sleeplike state is a condition of inactivity such as unconsciousness, dormancy, willful negligence and mental, emotional or spiritual blindness.

As with an alarm clock, the buzzing of a shake-up is annoying. In an attempt to awaken us, life will jolt us at a predetermined time and we will awaken with more knowledge and gratitude. This is considered a wake up call. But often when we are jolted we become distressed. We finally get up—but we are indignant, aloof, indifferent and uninspired. Other times we turn the alarm completely off, in an attempt to stay in our place of comfort—a mental position of denial, blaming, excuse making or inattentiveness.

Choosing to remain in the latter two conditions—readjusting ourselves to stay comfortable and unattached—gives life permission to pass us. When we finally experience momentary consciousness, we are shocked at how long we have actually been sleepwalking. Realizing that we have missed opportunity and advantage, we become weighted with guilt and remorse, and the cycle of excuses and blame takes place.

Our refusal to be in possession of our own lives and the "feel-good" of not being held accountable, provides the incentive for many of us to hit the snooze button (psychological denial and inattentiveness).

It would be easy for me to blame the many circumstances, pain and people in order to justify hitting the snooze button on my life, but I choose to own my stuff. What it boiled down to was my fear and unwillingness to be a conscious and responsible participant in my own life. I was more afraid of being judged and found wrong—than to live.

For a large portion of my life, I lived by four simple rules: First, anyone who held a position of authority knew what was best for me. Second, because of my distorted past, allowing me to be happy was mentally and emotionally risky. Third, I was to never ask for help: Asking for help would prove how weak I was. Fourth, I was to avoid making major decisions for my life. This spared me the pain of having my decisions weighed and found short. So when things went wrong I could remain safe and detached by blaming someone else. As you can imagine, this kind of toxic thinking guaranteed that my life would come falling down around me—and when it did, it wasn't a pretty sight.

Hitting the Snooze Button

While we would like to feel that we are aroused from sleep, consciously living and in charge of our lives, all we need to do is step back and take off the blinders. This one act would quickly reveal a very different reality—someone or something else was navigating our movements for us. Could this be the real reason for our psychological snooze buttons, to prevent waking up to find truth staring at us?

It is the stepping back, the *reflection*, that brings us face to face with how much and how often, we short-change our possibilities of a much richer life. It is this ability to reflect that makes us superior to all other living species, but along with this ability to reflect comes our ability to reason.

Reason is a mental state that gives explanation or justification to an action, decision or conviction. If our reflection, our recall, is negative, we are sure to experience exhaustive anxieties and these negative recalls affect our ability to reason. Mix the anxieties of negative reflection with distorted reasoning and you have a life of overwhelming limitations and restrictions. Allow that internal mixture to go unchallenged over a period and you have a professional sleepwalker, conditioned to hitting the snooze button in hopes of staying invulnerable to the revealed truths in life.

The moment we give ourselves permission to take a more participatory position in our lives, not the position of victim or bystander, but one of enterprising greatness, *reflection* transforms and becomes *guidance* and *reason* becomes *wisdom*. The two then act as valued and trusted internal advisors.

I remember the first time I began to view the ability to reflect as a positive gift and guide. I had left the United States, going to New Zealand. As I moved through customs, they ask three questions before permitting me entry into the country. Why are you here? Where are you going? And when will you leave?

At the time, the questions had little impact because I had other concerns of the unknown. It was not until returning to the United States that the same three questions, asked again in a different way, jolted one of those "shake-ups" in me. Where have you been? Why where you there? And where are you going now? These three questions became my "direction finders," my compass.

One reason most of us feel we have no control over our lives is we seldom give even the smallest thought of where we have been, why we were there and in what direction we now need to go. We are either in a constant automatic mode, reacting with knee-jerk responses, feeling that we have no power over the events and circumstances in our lives or we are in some mystic fog, believing God does not want us to participate, aim or have aspirations.

We use our snooze buttons as a protective mechanism to delay responsibility and pain, to avoid, to escape, to bargain and to deny where we have been and why we were there in the first place. Remaining asleep to these three questions will always keep us stuck, always looking to others to tell us what would be the best path for us to follow.

When I began to apply the first question to my life—where have you been?—repeatedly, as I wrote down brief descriptions of these places, emotionally and mentally, the response resulted in disappointment and pain. It was not until I began to utilize the second question—why were you there?—that I realized those places were not for pain, but for depth and breath of life. The message that I spoke and wrote would now leave my heart, reaching the hearts of others, something that would have never been possible without the lessons obtained in those places.

The misperceived advantage of the snooze button is its ability to act as a covering for our deeper issues of FEAR. Our fear of mistakes, success, rejection, negative recall and setting boundaries. Andrea Dworkin, feminist critic, said it best: "By the time we are *adults*, fear is as familiar to us as air. It is our element. We live in it, we inhale it, we exhale it and most of the time we do not even notice it. Instead of 'I am afraid' we say, 'I don't want to,' or 'I don't know how,' or 'I can't.'[1]

Self-permission in this area communicates a willful choice to give up our familiar lethargic state of comfort for a state of total wakefulness. A self-permitting that would allow us to give up the convenience of excuses, in order to participate fully in a resolve that would reveal to us clearly where we have been, why we where there and where we are to go.

Waking Up

Waking up means being aware of our environment, our own existence, our sensations, our thoughts. It means acknowledging our wants and needs as being valid. It calls for a constant state of mental perceptiveness that manages our emotional conduct and behavioral responses. None of which we can achieve without the power of self-permission. Our level of awareness will play a very significant role on our path to successful living. Our ability to stay cognizant along the journey will mean a great deal in determining whether we will entertain all of the possible detours, roadblocks and construction hazards along the way.

Because of our past, there will be a few things that will limit and obscure our wakefulness. For example:

We are in unknown territory

If we are truly in unfamiliar territory, every step will be a step of awkward faith. When we are inexperienced or unaccustomed to a particular thing or situation, we have no real point of reference, so how can we possibly expect to be sure or confident? We will be clumsy, ungraceful and clueless at times. However, this could present a gift of fresh learning and an opportunity to be attentive to our internal guide.

An African proverb states that many would rather live in familiar hells than to go to unknown heavens. Along with the comfort "familiar" provides for us, we also believe it will afford us greater advantages. Safe and secure does not require faith or excellence. It is when we move beyond the shores of what we have always relied upon that real greatness manifest itself.

The greatest example of finding richness in the unknown is in the book of Genesis. God told Abram, "Go for your self, for your own advantage, away from your country, from your relatives and your father's house, to the land that I will show you. There I will make you great, bless you and make your name famous."[2]

In those times of inexperience or blindness, we have a promise of guidance. A promise that leads in ways we have not known, that will guide us along unfamiliar paths. A promise that turns darkness to light before our very eyes and makes the rough places smooth.[3]

We are stuck on robot pilot and unaware we need to be aware

Directly or indirectly, our life's experiences program us to react to certain circumstances, situations and people without forethought or effort. Almost automatically, or by remote control, there are people and situations that just push our buttons. Like clockwork, like a mechanical device, we respond, often to our discredit, to the command of their agitations.

Waking up means refusing to blame our automated responses on our so-called difficult people or situations. It means challenging ourselves to identify what our emotional attachments are to a particular situation or person. Before anyone or anything can disturb or distress us, there has to be an emotional attachment or perceived emotional investment.

What I mean by emotional attachment or investment is, that we harbor emotional bonds, (ties, promises) affections, (soreness, prejudice) or loyalties (obligation, duty) to a negative past. At any time, an action, attitude, behavior, or situation can symbolize a negative event and it will cause us to regurgitate our time worn emotional or mental responses or fears. Our subconscious self will then communicate a need to protect, guard or attack and our self-sabotaging "Robot Pilot" switches to the "on" position and we move into reaction.

Life can grow weary when we fail to remember life's lessons

If a lesson is not adequately painful or important, the possibility of repeating that same unproductive behavior is greater. Unlike our present day educational system, the universe will keep us at a certain level in life until we reach required maturity. Failing to remember causes us to labor in vain, or to feel as if we are revving our engine and spinning our wheels going nowhere. Over a period, these repeated episodes or unlearned lessons will cause us to experience compounded injury and pain, which leads to a weariness of life, discontentment and bitterness.

A more important issue to remember about forgetting our lessons is it delays the inheritance of our intended purpose. As long as we are forgetting, we will fail to reach full development or maximum excellence. Forgetting leaves us in a state of immaturity, and all that is intended for us remains in the universe's trust fund.

We simply do not know any other way

This is a very common obstacle to our awareness and brings to mind a young woman who had attended one of my group coaching session where we were discussing the power of letting go of our excuses and other ingenious crutches.

She shared with us, with a voice of disappointment, that as a child she had learned to act less intelligent than her other siblings. This was her way of avoiding responsibilities, learning something new or receiving the attention she wanted. The adults in her life reinforced her behavior by openly excusing her actions with statements like, "Well, you know she's slow."

She went on to say she felt a sense of anxiety in realizing that she had been doing the same thing as an adult. Recently divorced after 17 years of marriage, reentering the workforce as a single parent, day-to-day pressures left her in deep depression. With a serious look of concern she said, "I have played the 'less than' role for so long, I don't know any other way."

Further discussion revealed that she was capable of many things but her experiences had taught her that acting helpless was better. Acting helpless meant getting the attention she wanted and diverted the rejection she didn't want.

Like this young woman, our lives have experienced many external changes, yet internally we remain the same—nestled comfortably in hibernation afraid to wake up and face the need for internal change. If we give ourselves permission to live the strength we hide, it would open us up to be more enterprising in nature as well as attract healthy attention. We would also find that the years of masquerading as helpless were a greater burden than living authentically. French author André Gide said, "It is better to be hated for what you are, than to be loved for something you are not.

Our unique ability to minimize and deny unfavorable results

This is selective memory or self-imposed amnesia used as a method of avoidance or escapism and produces a condition of staying stuck. When we minimize and deny results, especially negative results, we reject the opportunity to grow intellectually, spiritually and emotionally. This mindset keeps us safe from change and we are free to keep doing the same things in the same way, expecting a change, that they say, is insanity.

Minimizing, rationalizing or denying our hurts, anger, betrayal, fears and our need for security will only keep us prisoners within ourselves, or paralyzed to our life's opportunity. Acknowledging our fears or needs as valid neutralizes our internal critics. Notice I did not say, "*Accept*." I said, "*Acknowledge*." Two different things. If we accept negative emotions or situations, we receive it internally as a form of ownership. Acknowledging simply recognizes or admits the existence, which may express us but does not define us.

For those of us who are overly optimistic in nature, take care not to fall victim to the obstructions of "failing to remember life's lessons" and "minimizing results." We have a tendency to expect and dwell on the most hopeful aspects of a situation, which leaves us vulnerable to deception and mis-use. This also causes us to experience a life of exhausting effort with no result.

Phantom Visitation

Make no mistake: The phantoms or nightmares of our experiences will make it quite laborious to remain in an awakened state of mind. However, if we are prepared for their visitations, our future has the greater advantage. Being prepared means having forewarning of their visits and to scrutinize whether those visits are of punishment and affliction, or of comfort and blessings.

We have too much invested in the present to risk on the future

This occurs when we lack true self-definition and self-trust. When our worth and identity are dependent on our current positions, titles and situations, change of any kind will cause injury or cause us to feel vulnerable to loss. When the call of excellence sounds, some will readily take the journey to higher ground, but rarely do we voluntarily leave our place of safety by our own cognizance. For too many of us, settling for just enough is our greatest human error. We feel it's safer not to risk anticipating too much. If we don't anticipate or expect anything we won't be responsible to make decisions or change our lives and we won't have to risk being disappointed.

When we fail to give ourselves permission to move, to change, to grow, because of what we may lose, we live by the code of "The bird in my hand is worth more then those two in the bush." This fruitless mentality is one of scarcity that moves us to acts of greed, selfishness and desperation. It leaves us feeling that our investment of time spent in the familiar, no matter how toxic and uncomfortable, is far too valuable to exchange for an unknown place of promised delight and bliss.

The danger in accepting this illusion is that it causes us to bargain for the fate of our future. What do I mean? Many of us will never leave the comforts of the familiar unless we have been given an offer we just cannot refuse. At the time of the offer, we feel that we have just acquired the deal of the century, a win so advantageous—how could we ever lose. The irony of this limiting mindset is that it doesn't allow us to see beyond the short-term profit. While the offer initially has great appeal, and we go for what we see, over time the glamour and value diminishes and the cost to sustain it becomes greater than what we want to continue to pay in time, effort and commitment.

We dislike being uncomfortable

Our nature is that of comfort, convenience and instant gratification, so we gravitate naturally to a place of contentment, a place that does not require the full stretching of our abilities. When we truly seek to give ourselves permission, we realize that comfort, at least initially, is out of the question. During our transition, the place between "here" and "there," there will be temporary moments of aloneness, blindness, disorientation and awkwardness. These moments will cause us to reminisce and long for the comfortable. We will even hallucinate that the most toxic of situations and people were better than our present state of being in limbo.

This passage from a lower state and quality of mind and emotion to one of a higher degree will cause us to feel as though we are nomads—without a resting place or belonging. Truly understanding that these feelings are the cunning perceptions of loss comfort will allow us to stay the course. And staying the course is the simplest path.

We are afraid others will not accept us in our awakened state

For many of us "people pleasing" is a way of life. We believe that if we are not pleasing others, they will withhold their love and acceptance from us. Living a fictitious life of "less than" for the sake of not upsetting the ego or attitudes of others paralyses our movements in life. Giving ourselves permission to release these people to their own highest good so that our life can grow, will take conscious and determined effort. However, it is important to understand that an awakened state does not mean abandoning those we love and care for, it means nurturing their ability to be self-sufficient. This allows them the choice to become equal partners in the relationship and healthy relationships are based on reciprocity—a mutual, cooperative interchange of favors, privileges and respect.

We refuse to surrender

In this time of interrupting our status quo, making acquaintance with our authentic selves and being elevated from survival to significance, we will have more than enough time and opportunity to kick, scream, rebel and complain. If, however, we are committed to our success, my advice is to save your energy—you're standing still.

If there is one thing I have learned, refusing to surrender only prolongs the agony, delays movement and diminishes our confidence. When we give ourselves permission to embrace the changes and challenges along the path to success as lessons, we are able to put down our weapons of war and simply surrender our unnecessary control.

Author D.H. Lawrence once said, "If tonight my soul may find her peace in sleep and sink in good oblivion and in the morning wake like a new-opened flower then I have been dipped again in God and new-created."[4] Self-permission understands that there are times of needed surrender, of momentary rest, in order to let things take their course. Self-permission says: "Every fight is not my fight."

We lack even a 5% measure of faith

The "what if" (to the negative power) can be so strong at times that the very idea of being self-sufficient, competent and well appointed is amusing. When we lack a measure of internal faith in and for ourselves, we can always see success and opportunity for others, just never for ourselves.

This measure of faith that I speak of is a "believability" or confidence that knows: "Just because I can't see it now, doesn't mean it's not in the making." It is the same faith that plants a seed in the ground and knows with proper care, a flower will appear at its appointed time. This faith also knows that our planted flower will not arrive any sooner or any later then its time of maturity.

This faith can only be obtained through giving ourselves permission to *trust* the journey. It is a divine gift, a daily renewable attitude of trust and confidence in God's ability to work in and through us. In all honesty, this faith has absolutely nothing to do with our ability, but everything to do with God's sovereign capability to present us at the right time. What do we do in the mean time? Work the plan and believe—then believe and work the plan some more. Oprah Winfrey once said, "You have to work like it all depends on you and pray like it all depends on God."

Beyond Daydreaming

For years, we have been instructed to visualize our success, a better lifestyle, deeper relationships or a more fulfilling career, with minimal if any results. The problem is not in the method, but in the mental pre-condition of the visualizers. When our minds are accustomed to expecting little and hoping for even less, we cannot provide the environment to influence the growth, development and survival of our visions. This condition produces the question of '*how*,' and how is just '*confusion*' in a costume.

In an attempt to remain nestled in comfort, the subconscious will justify inactivity with feelings of displacement, confusion and misdirection. To our conscious mind, we believe we are being productive by trying to figure out "how to" bring something into reality. Being clear means decisions, action, change, resolution and commitment. Clarity moves us beyond daydreaming, to a place of action—risking exposure and judgment.

We are all familiar with Nike's action statement, "Just do it!" Great statement, and most of us will actually get a small buzz of hope every time we see the commercials or hear the statement. For a few brief seconds we wake up and contemplate the possibility of our dreams coming to life. Then comes the question that invariably follows the statement that ignited that awakening: "How do I start?" Within seconds, all thoughts and sensations become invalid and we sigh again in utter defeat, feeling it best to go back to sleep.

"How do I start?" is a question capable of causing an internal shakeup that repeatedly compels us to hit our trusted psychological snooze button. Better to keep sleeping than to face the insurmountable possibilities of failing, looking foolish, making a mistake or just plain feeling uncomfortable.

In the past, when workshop or seminar participants would ask me, "How do I start?" my reply was, "Just start right were you are." Over the years I have come to know, while this statement is partially correct, there is a major prerequisite required before any of us can "*just*," which will quickly move us to "*do it*."

The required prerequisite is what we have been and will continue to discuss throughout this book—self-permission, a power that holds with it a constant state of mental perceptiveness, emotional responsibility and behavioral accountability.

I truly believe that people do desire rich—successful lives. That is why we can go into any bookstore, turn on any television or radio, pick up any newspaper or magazine and get our share of five to twenty-five steps of "how to's." Canned, boxed or wrapped, we are not short of how to's in today's market of information.

Wonderful, but the biggest problem I have with 'how to's' is that it implies that 'one size fits all' and assumes every situation and person involved is relatively the same. Now, I am a woman and I know that one size DOES NOT fit all.

Using someone else's "*how's,*" sets us up for failure. What worked for one person does not necessarily guarantee similar results for another. Attempting to achieve success using another's pattern can be devastating, laborious and futile. "How to's" work very well for assembling things or developing a plan, but not lives—and certainly not hearts. Secondly, this approach is just another example of using someone else's permission, instead of our own.

I have found that successful living does not include collecting a laundry list of "how to's," but rather consists of being aware of and understanding the objectives of the word "How" in the question "How do I start?"

How is actually a *What* in disguise, with an objective of finding out our thoughts, feelings and desires. Say we have decided to want to wake up, to give ourselves permission. The first question many will ask is, "How do I start? Understanding the objectives of the word "how" says that our answer lies in asking:

- ✧ In what state or condition do I want to be mentally, physically, emotionally and spiritually?
- ✧ To what depth, degree or intensity of commitment will I give or go to achieve this?
- ✧ For what purpose or reason am I doing this?
- ✧ With what meaning, truth or significance will it have for me?
- ✧ What name, distinction or reputation will I want to identify me?

✧ By what standards will I perform and then measure myself?

Waking up to the "hows" in life is a collection of introspective "whats"—in what manner, what way and by what means. Once we have successfully completed the "what's," we will find ourselves going back to change or elaborate more on our earlier responses. This can happen immediately, a month or even a year later. The reason for this is: the clearer we become internally, the clearer and more focused all other things become.

I strongly suggest that we invest time in writing our responses down. Keeping it in our heads will merely allow it to be pushed back or overshadowed by other things. On the other hand, writing our responses down allows the mind to make room for more thought. It also allows our responses to become tangible—which moves us to take ownership and action.

No matter what our area of needed awakening, no two experiences will be the same. Once given permission, how, when and to what degree it happens would only be a guess. Of course, if we are serious about experiencing successful living, former President Ronald Reagan said it best: "No matter what time it is, wake me, even if it's in the middle of a Cabinet meeting."[5]

Permissive Power Challenge

Throughout the day, whenever you think of it, challenge yourself to have 5% more faith and trust in your purpose and intended direction.

As always, do not be concerned with what your purpose and direction may be, it will come. While focusing on obtaining your 5% increase, consider and answer the three "Direction Finders:"

1. Where have you been, emotionally and psychologically?
2. Why were you there?
3. Where are you going now?

Remember; there is no time span as to how long to challenge yourself and there are no pre-determined results or events.

3

The Issue Is Not that We Are Weak

"Self-reverence, self-knowledge, self-control.
These alone, lead life to sovereign power."
—Alfred Tennyson

We cannot talk about *permission* without discussing its rival, *forbiddance*. There is a struggle for superiority between these two very opposing exercises of the will. Although contentious in character, purpose and direction, their pursuit is the same—to be the benefactor of our hopes, desires and human qualities.

While one endows, strengthens and commissions, the other rules, controls and commands. One speaks possibility, the other impossibility. One offers freedom, the other prison, and the fate or condition of our life will rely on our commitment and our knowledge to choose.

You see, the issue in giving ourselves permission will not be that we are weak, but that we don't believe we are strong. Yet the key to this strength will be how much we are willing to permit and accept divine assistance and direction.

It has been my personal experience, as well as my experience in working with others, that we want to remove the restraints and limits in our lives. However, the depth of our belief patterns of forbiddance can be so overwhelming and controlling that we cannot comprehend the possibility of having the authority to choose.

In her book, *A Return to Love,* author Marianne Williamson said, "Our deepest fear is not that we are inadequate. Our deepest fear is that we are powerful beyond measure. It is our light, not our darkness, that frightens us." She went on to say, "There is nothing enlightened about shrinking so that other people won't feel insecure around you. We are born to make manifest the glory of God that is within us; it is not just in some of us—it's in everyone!"

"*Everyone*" in my dictionary means every person, everybody, the whole of humankind. If this is so, that everyone has a glory to discover and then to demonstrate for all to see, why aren't more of us (by our own intrinsic definition) living our brilliance? We being the glory of God strongly implies that no matter what level or status in life we presently find ourselves in, we have not yet reached our potential, because God's potentiality in us in unlimited.

The Iceberg Principle

Who can forget The RMS Titanic, a 46,000-ton luxury cruise liner that took its maiden voyage on April 10, 1912? For those who might have forgotten and others who vaguely knew the history, there was no forgetting, at least its splendor, after the release of the 1997 Oscar winning movie "Titanic."

The name alone denotes having great stature, enormous strength, power and influence, but who could have foreseen such massive loss and destruction of such a great and powerful vessel? Who could have foreseen the *ICEBERG*?

Allow me to feel as though I am about to educate you on the properties and facts of icebergs. I promise it will all come together before the chapter ends.

We all know the phrase, "just the tip of the iceberg." A metaphor that means what you are dealing with is deeper than it appears. This is literally true of an iceberg. Only 10% of its mass is above the surface. Its greater mass, 90%, is beneath the surface.

Icebergs come in all shapes and sizes and often are compared to the awesomeness of mountains, pyramids and castles. Molded by the actions of the wind and waves, their shapes are unusual and fascinating and the process of melting can change them even further.

The density of an iceberg is less than the density of seawater and this permits it to float. Although the wind affects the berg's movements, wind direction alone cannot judge its course. Because 90% of its mass is underwater, the currents have a greater affect on its movements than the wind.

No description could fit our properties and character as individuals, better than that of an iceberg. Like an iceberg, only 10% of our self—the image we want others to see—is above the surface. Our greater self, 90%, is beneath the surface, that part of us that is not directly evident.

My captivation with icebergs is the result of seeing one in a 3-D picture, "The Essence of Imagination," at a time when I wanted desperately to stop living my pains and disappointments. I had not yet comprehended the element of self-permission, so every day was a struggle, looking for someone or something to give me value and substance. One look at that picture and a revelation occurred that gave me resounding evidence that we are much deeper, much greater than we think or live. Wanting to understand our unseen 90% began my relationship with the "Iceberg Principle."

The concept of the human mind being compared to the anatomy of an iceberg was actually introduced in 1889 by Austrian physician and founder of psychoanalysis Sigmund Freud. He theorized that the unconscious self, which included strong sexual and aggressive drives, was a larger motivator of a person's behavior. Freud concluded that the human mind was like an iceberg: The small tip floating above the water was our conscious self and the greater part, our unconscious self, existed beneath the surface. He believed that although our unconscious motives could be suppressed, the suppression would only be temporary, because our unconscious desires and motives would find a way to be expressed.

Much of Freud's theory I disagree with, but I have come to respect his insight of using the properties of an iceberg to bring about clarity. I now use that same picture of an iceberg that caused me to consider our depth as humans in my seminars. And like Freud, my intent is to bring a clearer understanding that metaphorically describe our three dimensional selves, the conscious, sub-conscious and unconscious. It actualizes the magnitude and depth of our capacity to self-sabotage when internal channels are not clear. The devastation becomes greater when we refuse to permit our healing and elevation and instead resolve to live beneath our intended purpose. However, as we commit to self-work, that same picture becomes a visual stamp in our mind that bespeaks the depth of our splendor and mystique.

Just as the wind and waves affects the movement of an iceberg, life situations and circumstances affect us. However, situations and circumstances cannot judge or determine our life's course. What does judge, determine and affect our movements lies beneath our lofty outer appearances of fashion, education and titles.

I often say that what sank the Titanic was not the portion of the iceberg they saw. It was what they could not see. The same is true for us. What causes our greatest turmoil and hindrance is not what we see, it is what we do not want to see. As with the Titanic, we cannot comprehend the massive loss and destruction that our behavior and attitude can have on our life when our internal self is in a state of discordance.

Imagine for a moment we're an iceberg floating along in life. The 10% above the waterline is our conscious mind. The 10% that others see is our personality, image and behavior. Just below the waterline, at 60%, is our subconscious mind or subjective experiences, existing only in the experiencer's mind. Because the second dimension is the intangible self, others can only experience its lack or sufficiency through our actions and attitude. Just below the subconscious, extending even deeper below the waterline, at 30%, is our unconscious self. The unconsciousness is also intangible, rarely seen by others, unless the individual first discovers it and permits it to come forth.

Within the unconscious self is our endowment of power, our resourcefulness, our wisdom and truth. When we live from this level, we find our fullness of joy, our substance and intended purpose. From this level, we cease to crave, desire or long for the permission, approval or total acceptance of others—because we know that true permission, approval and acceptance lies only within us.

Now the question may be, if our unconscious self is our truer self, why does it make up a meager 30% of who we are? We are all born in God's image, of great stature, strength, power and influence. If the environment in which we develop and flourish provides support, guidance and nurture as we mature from error, poor choices and misgivings we will experience a 60% or even 70% truer imaging. However, if our environment is the opposite, the result is a 30% or less true image.

Here is the kicker in all this. Studies have shown that by the time we are 18 we will have been praised, supported and encouraged about 25,000 times, with 50% of these positive acts occurring by the age of 3. In addition, by the time, we are 18; we will be criticized, told off, humiliated, referred to as "stupid" and taunted about 225,000 times. You do the math: that is a 9 to 1 ratio of negative hits and if nothing occurs to challenge or correct those negatives, they take root and grow.

The reality is that we are subject to the weaknesses, imperfections and fragilities associated with being human. Add this fact to the many unnecessary external negatives that we so readily accept and welcome and, well, we become an emotional disaster in waiting. Our unconscious self will continue to be less than our subconscious self, until we willingly or by duress, reestablish a healthy internal relationship with ourselves. A relationship that learns, listens and loves the entire self, frailties and all.

This, sadly enough is our present day dilemma. All of our good stuff must somehow find its way pass our now injured subconscious self. If we would permit ourselves to look for the lessons our wounds and injuries hold, we would see our shaping and molding. Reassessing our injuries and wounds for their value allows us to realize things about ourselves we never knew before—and perhaps could never previously accept. When we find the lessons, we also find ourselves—a person full of prowess, of regal nobility, of splendor and authenticity, the real McCoy, the genuine article, with no illusions and no limitation.

This can happen if we give ourselves permission in two areas. First, by anticipating and granting a condition of wellness in our subconscious self. Secondly by giving more attention and trust to our unconscious self. And both must have our total commitment and desire to want something different. Swiss psychiatrist Carl Jung said: "The one who *looks outside*, dreams; the one who *looks inside*, awakens. Our visions will become clear only when we look into our own heart." What do you want, clarity or confusion, disorder or harmony, internal mayhem or balance?

Our need to commit to wanting something different reminds me of an inspiring occasion when Jesus healed a lame man who had been cripple for 38 years. When Jesus learned that he had been in that condition for such a long time he asked him, "Do you want to get well?" The man's subconscious pattern of lost hope and incompetence caused him to reply by placing blame on the external circumstances and situations.[6] The point here is, Jesus did not ask him about his external issues, he asked him about his internal want for wellness.

Because 90% of our substance goes unseen, our internal bearings (our predisposition of thought, action and behavior), healthy or unhealthy, will have a greater affect on our life than any external circumstance or situation. "A joyous, secure heart makes the face cheerful, but emotional wounds, defeatism, fatigue and mental torment crushes the spirit."[7] If we want to leave the place of lack, dryness, devastation and ruin, an internal "committed wanting" is crucial to the process otherwise all is in vain. This brings us to a subject worthy of discussion—"Wellness."

A Subject of Wellness

The American Heritage dictionary defines "Wellness" as a condition of good physical and mental health, especially when maintained by proper diet, exercise and habits. Recorded first in 1654, "wellness" has yet to receive the acceptance of its antonym "illness." In a recent survey, 68% found the word unacceptable when used in a sentence.[8]

What happens in the mind of a society that regards the term or condition "illness" as acceptable but finds "wellness" unacceptable? We are conditioned to give careful thought, consideration and attention to our lesser state of being. But to infer the possibility of an elevated state of wellness, well, that's just hogwash, crazy talk—a complete stretch of the imagination.

A mental and emotional state of wellness does not mean we have accepted the idealistic and impractical social theory of utopianism. It means that we stop the exhaustive acts of controlling and manipulating the will of others, which is our natural tendency, for the sake of empowering and governing ourselves. A quote worth repeating again by British poet Alfred Tennyson stresses,

"Self-reverence, self-knowledge, self-control;
These alone, lead life to sovereign power."

Permitting a condition of wellness means that we understand life or death is in our thoughts and spoken words. Every thought, every word has the potentiality of cursing or blessings, sickness or health, sadness or laughter. Wellness speaks loudly of the reverencing of self with honor, respect, adoration and benevolence. It is wholeness not reliant on the past emotional wounds, injuries or frailties that once characterized us. This wellness is probable, but will depend largely on how we view and value the significance of the word "deserve" vs. "worthy."

Deserve is to gain because of our behavior and efforts. Worthy is an inherent quality of excellence that commands esteem and respect, not dependent on behavior or performance. The word *inherent* indicates an immanent possession given by God. Worthiness is a divine gift given, not earned, and every human being has been given this endowment—with absolutely no exceptions. Giving ourselves permission to accept this great truth, as pure errorless fact, will take courage. To know that our worth is not dependent of our feeling worthy is critical to this resolve. Keep this in mind; even with the best of intentions, because of our experiences, our feelings are capable of misleading us.

The thought of permitting or accepting our worthiness as a gift will be a challenge because of our subconscious fascination with the concept of "deserving." Being able to accumulate often in the face of difficulties has a seductive affect on many. Being a victim or a survivor has great appeal to our psyche. Doing what comes easy or natural to us is not given high regard, because easy gets very little recognition. Our 60% subconscious that is stimulated by our past wounds and injuries, thrives to dote on our ability to suffer, causing us to believe that self-martyring brings greater honor and distinction.

When we permit wellness to occur in our 60% subconscious self, we begin the process of internal reconciliation. Reestablishing a closer relationship between our subconscious and unconscious self brings us to a wellness that will demonstrate stability and self-control. A self-control that is different from self-restriction and self-refusal.

Restriction keeps us confined within specified limits, small-minded and weak. Refusal is an unwillingness to accept or even to consider receiving something or someone. However, true self-control is the evidence of a balanced mind, a firmness of purpose, quietude of spirit, firm principles and self-ownership.

The Disputable Territory

In chapter one, I briefly detailed a battle from an episode of Star Wars between Luke Skywalker and his real archenemy. Like the character Skywalker, we are always ready to do battle with our perceived external enemies, the ones we see. Rarely are we conscious of the internal one who is hostile to our purposes or interests. Nor do we recognize when we are in an internal battle and that we may be fighting the wrong fight.

As I mentioned earlier in this chapter, two very real forces within us are at battle for superiority, to be the benefactor of our hopes, desires and human qualities. Remember the man who was crippled for 38 years, surrendering to the power of impossibility and becoming the prisoner of lost hope, incompetence and blame. His inability to experience healing was not an external issue—it was internal.

Remember this: life will always want to know how bad we want something. What are we willing to exchange for true success and life abundant? For this man, it was his bed of comfort and inactivity that had provided him with the unhealthy attention and pity of others.

Giving himself permission to acknowledge and take ownership of both his fears and true wants made possible completeness and a future unbridled. The level of our internal want for wellness will make all the difference in whether we will experience continuous wins or loses. Because this is a personal dispute within us, our hesitations will be very passionate at times. However, there still remains one resounding question, DO WE WANT TO GET WELL? Time has run out on blaming everybody and everything else for our lack and ills. Our life's success and fulfillments are too serious of an issue to continue with such nonsense.

For movement to begin, we must first permit ourselves to acknowledge that we are often operating with mythical beliefs as though they were facts. Whether we want to admit it or not, we all do, and the key is to recognize this and determine whether these beliefs are actual truth or fiction. At the very moment we experience any form of self-deprivation, the question immediately becomes, "Does this belief or thought represent actuality, or have I created it for protection, martyrdom, attention or self-pity?

The second thing we will have to acknowledge is that these negative beliefs will not just get bored and leave on their own. With absolutely no equivocation, they will have to be dislodged and removed. No friend, psychologist or drug can do this. Only the individual in whom it has taken residence can accomplish this. Once we extract these negative beliefs, we must do all we can to restructure our perceptions to be of sound quality and substance, lest the negative returns with greater vengeance—and the final condition is worse than the first.

There are three beliefs that are often mythic in nature, and their intent is to keep us bound in anguish, pain, guilt, doubt and fear. As long as we are in this kind of emotional or mental state of bondage, our life's purpose is destine to paralysis.

Mythical Belief #1
Success Means Being Alone

In one of my workshops, participants are ask to complete this statement with the first word that comes to their mind, "A powerful successful person is…" Their responses are words like arrogant, cold, self-involved, etc. On several occasions, I have had to ask for the positives of being successful. The participants respond, but the responses are much slower to come.

Having asked that question more than a hundred times during seminars and workshops, I will never forget the first time the statement was made, "A powerful, successful person is… and someone shouted "ALONE!" I was stunned. Never had I considered that success meant being alone, although a large portion of the participants had. They spoke of fearing abandonment, alienation, ostracism, rejection and exclusion. This caused me to ask the question: Is it aloneness or loneliness that we really fear?

Lonely often suggest a painful awareness of being alone, a grieving desire for companionship. This will be a psychological truth as long as we are living in the shadows of our emotional wounds and injuries. But as we move to a state of wholeness, we have to be careful not to let the temporary phase of aloneness to cause us to fear the gap between the old and the new. Otherwise, we will run the risk of acting in desperation. We must never lose sight of the truth that we are created for companionship. So there will always be relationships but there will also be the "gap" of advancing to new ones. Embracing our momentary periods of "aloneness" opens up the floodgates for healthier, more enriching relationships that will offer a greater sense of balance and growth.

Alone signifies being apart from others, but it does not necessarily imply unhappiness. Obtaining wellness will require separation from certain things, people or situations that prove to sabotage or hinder our success. There will also be those who will fall away once we are healthy—simply because they cannot control or manipulate our actions anymore. However, allowing ourselves to believe that aloneness is the price we pay for success or wellness is a myth created to protect us from our perceived fears of loneliness.

Mythical Belief #2
Our Past Heartaches Will Devour Us

A society of overindulgence has little tolerance for pain or grief. Our conditioning has taught us to anesthetize these sensations by synthetic external means. What solidifies this conditioning is our fixation, our obsession with imaging and aestheticism. We live by the doctrine that external beauty is the basic principle from which all other principles, especially moral ones, originate.

We dare not acknowledge, admit or talk about our emotional or mental torments or despair for fear of vulnerability or retaliation. Even in religious settings intended to offer the broken and contrite of heart refuge, pardon and reparation, we will find the greatest, most masterful of pretenders. If we grieve the loss of something or someone cherished, we are expected to "Get over it and move on" in as short a time as possible, because business must go on as usual.

We fight sorrow to an unusual extent. We think that if we release the lamentations of our heart or the pains we feel, they would devour or engulf us. Yet we never realize that the denial of them is much more devastating. Denying and rationalizing our heartaches may quiet the pain for a while, but at just the right moment, they will resurface to wreak havoc or paralyze us.

In our attempts not to be weakened or consumed by our pains, we silence and suppress them and become workaholics, perfectionists, stress magnets, victims and or casualties. When our internal cries become too loud, we hush or comfort them with pills, alcohol, cigarettes, sex and drugs. Maybe it's another bowl of ice cream, another job, another partner, another position, another car, another city, another and another and another, because we feel so unfulfilled. We will do anything and everything to avoid turning inward to hear the pain, to feel the pain and to forgive the pain.

Talking about or admitting to the emotional and mental injuries of betrayal or deception, what was snatched or stolen from us is initially painful. However, if we give ourselves permission to feel the full extent of those pains, not run from or silence them, the result is true long-lasting wellness.

I'm not suggesting that we began telling anyone who will listen all about our hurts and sorrows. What I do strongly encourage is that we began to converse with ourselves, turning inward to examine what lessons the pain and heartache want to teach us. To know what strength of character it is developing in us. To find out what emotional, mental or physical area is begging for our attention and nurturance. The belief that we are defenseless or inadequate in the face of our feelings is a myth that justifies self-imposed martyrdom.

Mythical Belief #3
We Are Our Emotional Injuries

It would be ludicrous to pretend that our emotional and mental injuries do not influence us. Even our physical body has a profound memory of all our past hurts and violations. Deep within us, time stands still, remembering every past event or occurrence as if it is still happening.

I will say this again: What causes our greatest turmoil and hindrance is not what we see, but what we do not want to see. Remember: Situations and circumstances cannot judge or determine our life's course. What does judge, determine and affect our movements lies beneath our artificial and papier-mâché fronts. Beneath our impressive appearances are the collective wounds and injuries that have become our identity.

The repeated violations of our emotions and the relentless pressures or resistance of life can be exhaustive and over time bring us to our knees. Our submission to the pressure moves us to believe that we and the emotional injuries are one in the same. This same defeatism will cause us to believe that wellness is for the special or favored—not for us. With every new experience or relationship, being filtered through our negative past our future is a self-fulfilling prophecy of failure or stolen opportunity.

This mind-set justifies our pessimistic outlook and allows us to live inferior or average lives. We have few if any expectations and we blame-shift to avoid being responsible, and we become the walking wounded. For many, this is a very attractive trade because, after all, what could possibly be expected from someone with such great injury? Why, my God, if we can just function with a reasonable degree of competence, that's more than can be expected. In fact, if nothing is expected of us, we never run the risk of facing failure, judgment or rejection.

As with the crippled man Jesus encountered who complained of his lack of opportunity, we too will complain in order to manipulate others by tugging at their sympathy to ensure rescue and assistance. We will even encircle ourselves with other wounded and injured souls as not to be challenged to change or to leave our bed of affliction. This in itself is the greatest of emotional violations.

Living, breathing, being our wounds echoes a life of deficiency. Our belief that weakness is more attractive than strength is a myth that justifies self-pity and validates negative attention.

In order to reclaim and bring our thoughts and beliefs into the captivity of truth over our many mythical beliefs, divine intervention is pivotal. Without this, the results of self-permission will be at best short-term and laborious, and at worst, the degeneration of character and action. However, before we can even begin to receive the effectual benefits of divine assistance, our "permission" is mandatory and our desire or "want to" is of a greater necessity. The reclaiming of our hopes, dreams and self comes by acknowledging that these beliefs, intended to change and spoil our form, are nonetheless ours.

Minimizing, rationalizing or denying these beliefs will only keep us prisoners within ourselves or paralyzed to our life's opportunity. Remember, acknowledging our fears or insecurities as valid neutralizes our internal critics and dissolves their strongholds.

Acknowledging simply recognizes or admits the existence, which may express us but does not define us.

The Flushing-Out

"All I ever wanted was to be as I once was—Unbounded.
Somewhere it got all twisted and before long sounded
as though life was a continuous connive-thrive-drive,
choking out the simple joy of just being alive."[9]
—Mary J. Blige

A life unbridled, not affected or restricted by the artful controlling of others and our internal fears is what we wish for—at least I do. Hip-Hop, R&B recording artist Mary J. Blige, spoke it with exactness: "To never seek again from man what God has chosen for us." To move beyond the never-ending episodes of conniving, thriving or driving for the next level of man-made imprisonments, disguised as success. That in itself would be an awesome accomplishment and to succeed at such a feat means invoking a self-permission that moves beyond our imposed limits.

The proper development of this self-permission is a process that starts with a "*beginning*." The beginning disassembles our games of pretense and prepares us for the proofing stages that establishes sound "*motives*" and "*intended purpose*." This process has a distinct element or quality about it not based on the opinions, attitudes and expectation of others. The process is intrinsically personal and very private, that is why I call it "*self-work*."

The Beginnings

"Beginnings" do not just happen—they are birthed. A birthing that comes when our internal essence is restless with being comfortable. A time that warns, "staying here means death by forbidden expression." In the "beginnings," no matter what our aim is, the intent of this place is to rediscover our potentiality, ableness and virtue. However, the first order of business is the disassembling of our fabricated personas, attitudes and realities; and so, what we have always known comes crashing down around us.

The greatest purpose for this crashing is for the disabling of our negative or contrived definition of life and self. This process breaks apart and challenges the unrealistic yet limiting "*supposed to be's*," in order for us to rediscover whom we ARE to be. In short, what the caterpillar calls *the end*, God calls a *butterfly*, and so starts the transition of one style developing into another, surpassing all limitations.

Becoming acquainted and sufficient in the act of self-permission will take time and will require a continuum of conscious living and accountability. "Beginnings" provide the conditioning necessary for us to develop and mature in the proper use of internal consenting.

In the initial stage of this developmental process, we will appear as a "Changeling," a changeable and fickle person, erratic in our actions and thoughts. "Beginnings" are simple and naive in style and they lack sophistication. Attempting to apply old abilities, attitudes and behaviors during this time will be very frustrating and disappointing. Its naïveté allows it to be free of past knowing. It will be as if we have a clean slate—whatever was, is no more.

In our beginnings, there are two principles to understand. First, there will be a part of us that will resist grasping this transition of consciousness as if our life depended on it. When we have lived a life accustomed to being lead or asking permission, our very being sees anything else as treason. Therefore, until we become more secure in the act of giving ourselves permission, our internal resistance is inevitable. Bouts of regression and relapses are just part of the process.

Secondly, our attitude will be very important on the other side of "beginnings." When we emerge, will our disposition be one of anger, presenting gifts to assure your acceptance or wanting reverence? For the sake of our arrival, it is extremely important that we understand there are really no beginnings and no endings—there is only movement. This means that no matter what happens in a day, win, lose, or draw, we have another opportunity and another and even another, to stop and begin again correctly. Henry Ford said, "Failure is the opportunity to begin again, more intelligently."

When we recognize and acknowledge where we may have slipped, we have not lost ground, we have gained knowledge and we are still moving. By bringing healthy knowledge forward, we can always, always reset the shot clock and keep possession of the ball. We forfeit only when we deny our imperfections and error as a necessary part of growth.

So what—if our internal voice of negative recall got the best of us that moment or that day. The key here is to understand that past moments, past days are no longer in time. We have the greater advantage because we have "right now," we can set the counter back to zero and go at it again. By adapting this mindset, the mental "*what if's*" to the negative power and screams of failure cannot move us to recede or withdraw. It absolutely releases us from remorse, shame and guilt and propels us into a consciousness of constant forgiveness of self and others. It is not what happens to us, but what happens in us that wins the war.

Becoming acquainted and sufficient in the "beginnings" of self-permission will take time, so tenacity and perseverance is paramount.

Proofing Motives

Somewhere in our beginnings, the proofing of our motives will commence. This second stage is not only to prove the state of our motives; the intent is to make corrections. Proofing offers an opportunity to start again, not in old ways but with a conscience of newness. With more intelligence, greater integrity, being more discriminative, with greater quality of character and with objectives that are more solid.

Proofing allows us to examine our motives and our character. It allows us the unadulterated opportunity to finally ask, "Who am I really, outside of all the manipulations and expectations of others?"

Our motives for refusing to give ourselves permission may come from the benefits we believe exist when others have greater authority in our lives. When another is in charge of our life, it allows us to avoid the anguish of making a decision and through blame or excuses, we will always have an out. Allowing someone else to have control enables us to maintain our pseudo-persona of superiority because we escape the judgment seat. It also allows us the advantage of remaining the victim in order to manipulate others through guilt.

Others will refuse the power of giving themselves permission because it would mean looking deep within the self at our true driving forces, guiding principles and real beliefs. Acknowledging that our motives are of selfish-ambition, oppression, or narcissism, would remove our excuses and justifications. In all honesty, when I realized that the strength of permission was so powerful, I could see why some avoid it, others want to control it and still others manipulate and connive for it. The greatest feeling of supremacy is in knowing that you control the thoughts, moods, actions and attitudes of another.

Self-permission restores our power of granting and consenting. However, this act of empowerment requires conscious accountability for our words and actions, as well as a strong commitment to motive and integrity. Scripture says we fight, desire and crave to have and cannot obtain because we do not expect, seek or inquire. And when we do, we do not receive because we expect, seek or inquire wrongly.[10] Which means our self-permissive power is improper, defective or used in a careless way—an issue of motive and integrity.

Let me clarify this further. **Improperly** means that we may be expecting or seeking with an unpleasant attitude or an attitude of entitlement. **Defective** implies, we have ulterior motives or hidden agendas, or our granting is impulsive, without real forethought. This is a form of spontaneity, which can be invigorating; but spontaneity out of control can be chaotic, stressful and quite devastating. **Carelessness** communicates that we are without clear consideration and respect to our own and that of another's true destiny and purpose. It can also reveal that without proper development we can be mislead, misinformed and manipulated by self or others.

This stage of proofing is of great importance. It promotes the surfacing of our improper, defective or careless motives for the sake of restructuring and developing strong integrity in our future use of self-permission. Along with reestablishing greater quality of character and solid objectives, there are four opportunities for deep introspection

The first opportunity of self-study will be to embrace solitary travel, a journey of aloneness that excludes external distractions and allows the inner voice to be more audible. This aloneness stresses being apart from the nonaffirming opinions and behaviors of others, and if properly embraced the excitement of rediscovered abilities and strength will emerge.

Initially our internal voice will be both negative and positive. The proofing enables us to recognize which is truth. Swiss psychiatrist Carl Jung says, "We must be alone to discover what supports us when we can no longer support ourselves. Only aloneness gives us an indestructible foundation." Secondly, we have an opportunity to rewrite our life's script, mentally, emotionally and physically. You see, we cannot go back and change our life's start, but we can change at our present point and begin again to build our future.

Thirdly, this becomes an awesome opportunity to discover what we really want. Not what someone told us we could have, as a form of granting a favor, but what we deeply desire. And fourth, to honestly consider the regret we will harbor if our life is not lived fully. Maslow's Hierarchy of Needs theorizes that refusing or blocking the gratification of a human spirit moving towards growth and self-actualization causes internal ruin, injury and pain.

We may secretly desire to be in the spot light or to be openly recognized for a particular talent but because of social and mental conditioning we deny it. But the sooner we acknowledge and take ownership of our hidden desires, the sooner the universe can bring them into proper balance. Our desires are for purpose, giving ourselves permission to free them, sets the stage for them to be proofed for appropriate use—anything less is self-betrayal.

"Twenty years from now you will be more disappointed by the things that you didn't do than by the ones you did do. So throw off the bowlines. Sail away from the safe harbor. Catch the trade winds in you sails. Explore, Dream and Discover."
—Mark Twain

I would truly have to admit that one of the greatest pains I think a human spirit can experience is the pain of "regret." To get to the end and face knowing that we denied our intended purpose—that would be devastating.

Proofing Intended Purpose

The third stage of proofing is one of resolve and certainty. If there is one reason our lives are short-changed, it would be because we fail to be deliberate and intentional—to live on purpose!

Who am I, what is my purpose, where do I fit in? These questions are constant, especially in young people today. As a society, we are faced with a mindset of disorientation and role confusion. Because of conflicting pressures and expectations, which often produce acute anxiety, we are looking at a future of unreadiness. Knowing the intentions of our life's existence is like having possession of our identification papers; it validates our core meaning.

As with our motives, our intended "purpose" will also require proofing in order to introduce us to our authentic identity of being. Disabling our imposter complex and our negative self-imagining eliminates the stress and reluctancy of self-permission. However, knowing our intended "purpose" can strike fear in the best of us, because it causes us to take ownership of our reactions or lack of action. Our fears can include making a mistake, perceived inadequacy, negative recall, maintaining a perfectionist status, fearing judgment, lack of resources and much more.

Intention is simply a committed course of action that one proposes to follow, but the intentions that govern life have purpose, honor and meaning. When what is "intended" has permission to breath and is empowered with purpose and aim, the effect is awe-inspiring.

Purpose strengthens the intended with unshakable faith and determination. *Aim* stresses the specific direction our intended efforts will take in pursuit of our desired goals. The proofing that began with our motives enables us to see more clearly our intended purpose.

When we deny our intended "purpose" permission, we risk not having clear, concise direction. We live with a fear of not being acceptable or adequate to have significance. In addition, if and when we do achieve a measure of success, we either feel it was luck or we are suspicious as to how long it will be before things come crumbling down around us.

By not giving our "purpose" permission to manifest itself, we are subjected to the dictates of others. I believe when we don't know our own direction someone else will give us their direction—and this is a phenomenon that happens far too frequently. Withholding permission from our "purpose" only enslaves us to the day-to-day roller coaster attitudes, behaviors and opinions of others, which leaves us unbalanced, bewildered and confused—and that, my friend, is by design. Because confusion delays as well as denies movement.

The objective of proofing our intended purpose is to clarify the distinction between our true path and the suggested paths of others. Its objective is to become so interchangeable, so indistinguishable that our total being—mind, will and emotions—becomes inseparable of that purpose.

Purpose allows us to aim well towards our life's goal and then assures we hit the mark. This is where we can best utilize the answers to our three questions of direction in Chapter 2. Where have you been, emotionally and psychologically? Why were you there? Where are you going now? This proofing will also allow us to define more precisely, the what's of our "How"(Chapter 2).

There will be many other barriers of perception and emotion attempting to restrict our self-permissive power and success.

Nevertheless, if we remain diligent and committed to ourselves, we may not recognize and divert all of them, but we will recognize a large portion of them. Once we recognize these barriers, knowing our purpose will obligate us to permit our necessary character corrections.

Again, it is not my intent to change minds, but to challenge the comfort of our present mind-set. To allow the mind to do what it does best—think, reason and apply knowledge.

Permissive Power Challenge

Throughout the day, whenever you think of it, challenge yourself to have 5% more faith and trust in your intrinsic strength. As always, do not be concerned with what you have felt about yourself in the past. This is about your future. Your immanence is not about how you feel, but about deep-rooted internal fact.

Remember; there is no time span as to how long to challenge you and there are no pre-determined results or events. Just let this one happen.

4

Success Is A Tapestry

"Success is the American Dream we can keep dreaming because most people in most places, including thirty million of ourselves, live wide awake in the terrible reality of poverty."[11]
—*Ursula K. LeGuin*

During a regional sales conference, one of the participants shared with me a stressful situation she was experiencing with one of the company's sales training managers. She had been with the company for over a year and her sales were a little above average. She enjoyed her professional path in sales, but was now experiencing some difficulties that were affecting her livelihood. Although her position provided a base salary, the majority of her income came from the commissions she earned from sales.

Her stresses started when the sales manager ask her out to lunch. Accepting the invitation, the sales manager suggested accompanying her to visit with her last prospective client and from there, they would go to lunch. The young woman said they had an enjoyable lunch and afterward thought nothing of it, until she received e-mail from the manager stating that she would be receiving her performance evaluation in a few days. She admitted feeling somewhat offended by the sneak-evaluation technique, but still thought nothing of it. After receiving the written evaluation, she was literally stunned.

The sales manager had evaluated her performance as needing great improvement and suggested she adapt the selling techniques of one of the company's top seller. For more than a week, she agonized over why her method was in such error. Deciding to take the criticism in stride, she began implementing the suggested techniques, although she felt it didn't fit her particular style or personality. The first week she experienced a drastic reduction in sales, which of course affected her commission. Feeling she just needed to get use to the new system, she continued the following week with the same techniques—but sales continued to decline. By the third week, she was feeling the pressure and stresses of being a failure, as well as being racked with grief over abandoning her own method.

I suggested that the young woman look over the new techniques carefully and select those things that truly fit her personality. If the entire method didn't work, it was possible that portions of it might. If none applied, she was to literally write down her method step by step. Once that was completed, she was to look at her method, decide what areas of the process she really enjoyed and become more animated and personable in those areas. In the other areas she was to decide what she could do to be more effective, either by practicing more in the mirror, having more knowledge of the client or gaining greater knowledge of the product to add variants of value and benefit to the client.

Two weeks later, the young woman called to report that she had returned to her own selling techniques, but had added animation and greater product knowledge to her method, and was having a ball. She went on to report that sales were going very well and she had since closed on several large accounts, almost tripling her previous high.

Her sales manager made the error in judgment that many well-meaning on-lookers do—if a method of success works for one, it will work for all. Many believe that there is only one way, only one path to success. So instead of brainstorming on ways to improve or strengthen individual techniques, they choose to fit everything and everyone in a tried and proven form. A Chinese proverb says, "There are many paths to the top of the mountain, but the view is always the same." While the results of success may look the same, the paths to that end are quite different. When we allow ourselves to see success from a cookie-cutter perspective, we are actually short-changing our own success.

Success, like *permission,* is a word of action. Where permission is an action of granted power, success is an action of realization and completion. The result of this action is favor, notability, mental and emotional well-being, affluence and economic prosperity, just to name a few. From this perspective, success is the same, but when we see the act of accomplishing success as one-dimensional, we are not seeing it at all. Like a fine tapestry, success is made up of a combination of its many intricate parts that are difficult to follow or analyze except by its creator.

Therefore, we can set aside any attempts to put success in a definable box of specifics. Real success is self-styled; it is as unique as the individual who achieves it. Success is an art that communicates the ideas and inner expressions of its creator, giving him or her the opportunity to experience the virtue of being a surrealist.

In the early 20th century, a group of writers and artist dared to express their works from a place of subconscious uniqueness. They referred to this movement as *surrealism.* This movement demanded that human creativity be outside the box of what the societal dictates said was proper and acceptable. Their movement was that of giving themselves permission to trust their inner expressions over the established external boundaries.

The secret of experiencing this professional euphoria lies completely in doing what we truly enjoy. However, in order to know the joy that would bring us success, we have to know first, who *we* really are. But for many of us, the cart has come before the horse. We live daily torn between what we should do, what we think we want to do and what others say we ought to do. We exert large amounts of time and energy on a quest to find out what our "purpose of doing" is, which to many remains elusive. The problem is not that we have no purpose of "doing," the problem is that our energy is focused on the wrong character of *purpose.* Our true focus is to be on our "purpose of being"

When we seek to clarify our "purpose of being," we will inevitably discover our "purpose of doing." Let me bring this thought to life. Our position of "doing" says that we produce and then execute. It is a behavior, a conduct or a performance. "Being," on the other hand, is to belong or exist in "fact," with specified significance, quality and character.

Allow me to expound on this "fact." Some years ago, I made acquaintance with a Pastor from Cincinnati, Ohio. Over breakfast, we were discussing my struggles with the traditional form of reaching the hearts of people through ministry. There was much wisdom shared with me that morning. But there was one statement of instruction directed totally to me as a person. He said, "Pennie, my instruction to you is to *BE*." I pulled on his intelligence and wisdom to tell me what he meant by "*BE*" but he only replied that that was all he could tell me. As you can imagine this forced me to figure out what he meant—here is what I found. To "Be" says that we are: *actual, real, essential, substantial, present-day, latter-day, the latest, well-thought-out, self-consistent, full of substance and phenomenal truth*. His instruction that day was for me to live—to "be" these things and success would manifest itself naturally—beautifully. My challenge was to give myself permission to acknowledge, accept and own my being.

In our obsession to "fit in," by *doing*, we cast aside the very thing that makes us worthy of notice—our uniqueness—our *being*. There are thousands upon thousands of undiscovered, uncelebrated highly intelligent and talented individuals (she is talking to me too) in this world. Yet, if we were to ask why our internal greatness goes unseen, unheard and unexperienced, many would not be able to articulate, nor are we able to fully comprehend, the internal oppositions that so fervently plague us. Our self-imagery is so imbalanced that when others recognize our activities, we superbly discredit, minimize, devalue and disown our abilities and contributions. While we may think that we are being humble, what we're actually doing is teaching others not to appreciate us.

A colleague once told me that the climb to success had three levels: Survival to Stability, Stability to Success and Success to Significance. She went on to assure me that I was at the second level moving steadily towards the third stage. Since I was in a particularly grim time in my life, mentally, emotionally and financially, I refuted her analysis, saying I was clearly at the first level struggling to survive. The more she pointed to my personal attributes and skills, the more I questioned their value and her sensibility.

Weeks after that conversation, I found myself emotionally exhausted over my many failed attempts for success, professionally and relationally, so I decided to go for a power walk. With the temperature nice and the wind strong, I felt that would be a good way to blow out the cobwebs in my head and regain some sense of direction.

Ten minutes into the walk, I realized I was huffing and walking as if I was going to war. I knew at that point that it was more than just a power-walk. I was walking out some issues, and one of those issues was with God. So I decided to permit myself to set aside all my learned taboos and rituals about how we should interact with God and just have my say.

"Okay God, you said in your word that you show no partiality; with you, one person is no different from another.[12] So I want to know why is it that I have been at this success thing for a greater portion of my life and I keep finding myself at floor zero. I see people half my age and they are successful, so what is your issue with me? I am tried of people telling me you'll be all right, you're a survivor. To be perfectly honest, God, I am exhausted with merely surviving. I want to live and live abundantly. Now I need to know what's wrong here!"

Mind you, I was still huffing out this walk, angry, mouth stuck out and all. My pace slowed as I attempted to hear my internal voice with his reply, but received nothing. Weeks later revelation surfaced an agonizing answer that I was not quit ready to acknowledge. The real offender of my success was none other than my flawed definitions and beliefs and my lack of self-value and confidence.

Giving ourselves permission to live inside the ideas of our inner expressions—our being—employs a self-assertion that reclaims our right to acknowledge and take ownership of our intelligence and talents. It beckons us to leave the safe conditions of a colorless life for temporary feelings of displacement—and the pure awkwardness associated with success. Unfortunately, instead of giving ourselves permission to live inside the power of our creativity, we relinquish it based on our stresses and fears about success. There will be more than enough distractions, and we will have to recognize these diversions even when they are self-induced. The following mental attitudes can certainly be considered self-induced diversions, and can predetermine our responses as well as our interpretations of personal success.

Being in competition with the wrong person. We spend countless hours strategizing how to gain advantage over another person. We will lose sleep rehearsing and studying the game plan. When we consume ourselves with competing with another person, we have misplaced our focus. The key to being successful at anything is to acquire selective vision, giving our attention to only what enhances or nourishes our goals—personally and professionally. The only competition we need to engage in, is challenging ourselves to bring forth more inner qualities today than yesterday, and positioning ourselves for even greater exposure tomorrow.

Comparing or defining our successes by the standards of others. Success is relative. Or as I said earlier, it is a tapestry rich with many intricate parts that cannot be analyzed except by its creator. Comparing ourselves to another in any area of life is the greatest weapon against personal success. Believing that our path to success will be as hard or as easy, as wonderful or as disastrous as another's, will not only limit our awareness, it will also cause us unwarranted apprehension and stress. Comparing—defining our success by the standards of others—will cause great bouts of depression and personal putdowns. Our success may have similarities but are never equal, never identical. French author André Gide said, "*Man* is more interesting than men. God made *him* and not them in his image. Each *one* is more precious than all."[13]

Lacking the courage to look foolish for the sake of our goals. Boy, do I know this obstructing mental attitude. If we wrestle with perfectionism, struggle with personal confidence or fear rejection and judgment, the possibilities of looking foolish will cause us to abort a doable plan. The possibility of appearing awkward or unskilled is common with any new task, even with the best preparation. Many think that confidence and excellence just happen. Only through repetition—and error—does confidence take root and excellence become visible. It is in our moments of awkwardness or inexperience that success becomes a teacher. But when we can't comprehend our success we can't learn from it, and looking foolish is not a fair tradeoff. However, keep in mind that some of the craziest ideas have brought the greatest results—probably because no one is suspicious of "crazy."

Believing that we are a hoax. Because of our attitudes and issues of being "*deserving*" or "*worthy,*" many live with the internal agony of others finding them to be a fraud—a hoax. Many intelligent, competent go getters accuse themselves of being a trickster. We think, "If anybody ever found out, how much of a hoax I am, I would be out of here." With the anxiety of being discovered as a fraud comes our need to keep relationships at a distance or to keep them superficial. In her book, 'The Imposter Phenomenon,' Dr. Pauline Clance found that those who experience this phenomenon secretly believe that others have overestimated them and, in time, the truth will come out and life will be ruined. She notes that 70% of all successful individuals suffer from an imposter's complex—70%.

Because of these and many other self-induced diversions, it is very important that we possess a strong sense of character. You see, when we attempt to project an image of success that we really don't believe, it will feel fraudulent. So our character (our attributes, traits and abilities) must be developed. I truly believe the success of the surrealism movement hinged on the artists knowing, and understanding who they really were and wanting to express that realness. I would also be willing to bet that a quality of character emerged in each participating individual during the course of events and actions that took place.

Challenging the status quo or the societal dictates of today will demand no less from us than they did centuries ago. While we have the luxury of enjoying the fruits of this early 20th-century uprise (the variants of success), we must still develop a strong combination of personal qualities. If we desire long-lived, self-styled success, we will have to undergo a process of development that is non-negotiable. Our area of development will be in that of a durable attitude, definable skills, a fortified character and the willingness to invest in ourselves.

Durable Attitude

A "durable attitude" means being capable of withstanding wear and tear. It does not mean we disconnect with the realities of the events, issues and people in our world. It means just the opposite. A durable attitude is a healthy attitude that says, "I choose to be more consciously discriminative as to who and what I allow to dictate the "mood of my day or life." A healthy attitude understands it's not about how often we get knock down or detoured in life, it is how long we choose to stay down.

For those who do not yet possess this durability, those who choose not to be involved with self-work (introspective digging), may view the durable as selfish, unconcerned or arrogant. Some even choose to believe that those who do have healthy, durable attitudes have never experienced true hardship and pain.

In defense of the durable, in fact, it is the hardships and the pains that have actually caused them to seek out a way to rise above the muck and mire of life and to develop the attitude and perception of an achiever. Instead of focusing on and magnifying the negatives of their temporary condition, they permit themselves to focus on identifying the lesson they are to learn. In doing so, they create an internal stability that stands up to possible deterioration.

Achievers give themselves permission to forget the lyrics of their favorite "*somebody done me wrong*" songs. They take off their pity party hats and they commit to action despite any perceived difficulties, all for the sake of their awaiting future.

A note to the not yet durable: Until we are willing to labor in our self-work, dispelling some of the junk we mistakenly accepted as truth, the successes of others will always cause us to suffer resentment and envy. It will limit us within the teams, partnerships or groups in which we participate. And we will always wish in vain and chase aimlessly after an experience of success that constantly eludes us or is short-lived.

Because our success is self-styled, nothing can be more devastating to it then self-deprecation inherited from, self-induced or infected by another. Pilots know too well the importance of attitude. Every aircraft is equipped with an instrument called an "attitude indicator." Its function is to gauge the position of the aircraft in relation to a particular reference line, such as the horizon. If the aircraft's attitude is dysfunctional and focused on the wrong line of reference, the craft faces sure destruction.

Our attitude is the reflection or carrier of our internal valuing system, known as "*esteem.*" As in the aircraft, if we align our internal selves with the wrong line of reference, we too will be headed for destruction. Therefore, guard your attitude, for it expresses to others your internal durability.

Definable Skills

Most of us are guilty of observing our world and events with one-dimensional sight, believing, seeing, defining in terms of "only."

We look at having a "skill" in the same way, identifying it only as some form of performance, exchange or knowledge that one has learned or acquired. However, I see skill, true skill, as being three-dimensional. On the surface, it is performance, exchange or knowledge. The second level however, is an expression of imagination, intelligence, touch and conduct. The third level is the intrinsic possession of a gift, an endowment of power, virtue and authority.

When we look at skill as an acquired learning, instead of an internal possessing, we will never be the owner of confidence. This mindset makes us an easy target for anyone who is egotistical. It becomes easy to feel inadequate, challenged, threatened or intimidated in the company of another who understands the internal ownership of their skills—and the ability to permit others to experience those skills.

This third level insight is deeper than most of us are consciously aware. Some of us stumbled upon this knowing. Others possessed a character that demanded this knowing come forth. Still others gained their insight by being in environments that allowed error and the feeling of safety to try again for the sake of internal and external progress.

In my years as a personal success educator, I have asked countless participants to pair up with another person and, within 30 seconds share their dominant gift and or talent. Repeatedly, a large percentage would either shrug their shoulders, claiming not to have any, or they would throw something out that someone told them they were good at and then use the remaining 20 seconds to brag about the abilities and talents of a loved one or friend.

As I would watch these different groups struggle with the simple act of being aware of and claiming their gifts and talents, it became evident that most of us either do not believe we have skills or we don't take ownership of the skills we are aware of. Nick Williams said it best in his book, *The Work We Were Born to Do*, "The ego is so clever—what better place to put our gifts than in a place that we are scared to go—our own internal self."

I hope you recognized that I preceded the sub-title word *skill* with the word *definable*. By this, I mean that once you permit yourself to identify, acknowledge and own your skill, the next phase is to make those skills distinctive of you.

What do I mean? Because you now understand this "internal possessing," there is now a requirement to do more than just own it. It becomes a strong requirement to specialize it, set it apart, to make it eminent, towering or standing out above all others. Not in a way as to compete or prove—but as an offering of internal excellence. This offering becomes an artful demonstration or signature that says, "When others experience me doing what I do, they know I DO THIS!"

A better way to view this is to let your definable skill touch others. It's been said that people will forget what you say, they will forget what you did, but the will never forget how you made them feel—always, leave them with a good feeling.

Fortified Character

"The common idea that success spoils people by making them vain, egotistic, and self-complacent is erroneous; on the contrary, it makes them, for the most part, humble, tolerant and kind. Failure makes people cruel and bitter."[14]

—W. Somerset Maugham

Something that is a constant soapbox discussion for me is the degree of urgency and awarded compensation our society puts on the first level of skill: performance, exchange or knowledge. With this also comes the demanded expectation to be able to perform these skills with the intensity and vigor of a Super Hero. This demand also has little concern has to how and by what means the end results are obtained.

A portion of being successful does mean being visible, obtaining an audience, being a mover and a shaker, generating and motivating results. However, how and under what conditions or means we achieve this is a vital part of experiencing rich and significant success.

As a young woman, I remember my grandmother insisting that we have good posture. She would have us walk around balancing books on our heads. She was very strict when it came to understanding and honoring the rules and laws of ladyship.

Make no mistake, to her, upholding a certain outwardly image was very important. There were plenty times that I wanted to be a tomboy and would become intolerable with my "whys." "Why can't I just go like this? Why do I have to come down from the tree? Why do I have to wear these gloves? Without ever raising her voice she would snap, "It is important to look good. Nobody will ever know how silly you are until you open your mouth, so you have to look good!" I also remember her referring to people who I perceived to be polished and of quality as "All front and no back." It would be years later when I grasped the concept that *STYLE* plus *SUBSTANCE* equals *QUALITY* in a person.

Our actions of character will always verbalize and define us, even when we have not spoken a word. The adage is, "What you do speaks so loud, I can't hear what you are saying." While we are able to give stellar performances of pretended qualitative character, under pressure, when we least expect it and usually do not want it, our true character always emerges.

Character improperly fueled, or lacking emotional, moral and mental strength, over time will reveal a more truthful account of who we really are, through greed, vanity or fear. A reflection that will communicate a person who is superficial, immature, unreliable, temperamental, compromising, unstable, contemptible, hateful and demoralized.

Shaping or establishing a fortified character takes great courage and discipline. Courage, because we will have to give ourselves permission to release all behaviors and attitudes meant to suppress our fears—and to refuse the temptation to use any and all past tricks and schemes in order to achieve or get ahead. It will take discipline because self-permission decides to walk through the fire, instead of conniving or bargaining an easier way around it. Success in this area will depend strongly on our ability to permit divine intervention and support to take place. Without the element of divine management, our character will remain masked with hidden distortions and agendas.

No matter how great we think we are, we all have characters that are in need of strengthening. We are all born with an instinctive nature to do wrong. Studies have shown that while we do have to teach our children the values of truth and honesty, we do not have to teach them how to lie, sneak or cheat. Our nature will also initially resist anything contrary to its instinct to survive.

Helen Keller experienced this when faced with the need to fortify her character. Once she came out on the other side she wrote, "Character cannot be developed in ease and quiet. Only through experiences of trial and suffering can the soul be strengthen, vision cleared, ambition inspired and success achieved."

The Willingness to Invest in Yourself

As previously mentioned, the one thing that makes us superior over all other living things is our ability to reflect. To meditate, weigh and examine our past actions and conduct for the sake of learning and growth. Therefore, for the sake of establishing the importance of the last intricate part of your self-styled tapestry of success, I want to reflect on a time that caused me great internal pain, but nonetheless became a teacher that engaged me to fight for my self-permissive power.

I had just come out of a toxic relationship that had left me in shambles emotionally, mentally, spiritually and financially. For the third time, I had found myself again rummaging through the shattered pieces of my life, hoping to find something of myself that was salvageable. With each destructive episode, the losses of self and property become greater and I was living a life that was past being on empty.

This particular night, my daughter and I were driving down the highway and I was in rare form, wearing my pity party gear and singing loud and strong my "*somebody done me wrong song*."

Its often been said, when the student is ready, the teacher appears. Well, on this night the teacher appeared in the voice of my daughter. Go with me while I reflect on the conversation that took place that painful, yet wonderful night.

"Mom, I really need to talk to you about something."

In what had become my usual irritated voice I said, "NOW what's wrong?"

"Nothing is wrong, I just want to talk to you about something I have observed about you and I am concerned about it."

Again, in an irritated voice I say, "Well what is it?"

"Now, mom, I'm not saying this to hurt your feelings, so don't think I'm saying this to rub salt in the wound."

“Okay, okay, get on with it.”

“You promise not to get mad?”

Exhaling loudly, “Okay, I promise. Will you just get on with it?”

There was a moment of complete silence. Then, “Mom, you have been there for LeAlec and I and we love you for that. When the children’s father went south on me, you were there. Over the years, I have watched you risk everything you have on everybody else, the men, your family, friends, you have even paid people who did not deserve to be paid—just accepting their poor work that you couldn’t even use. Now, what do you have—nothing, it’s all gone and where are they?

Truth is in my face and it is beginning to hurt. Gritting my teeth in an attempt to repress the angry, I said, “So what are you trying to say?”

“Mom,” she exhales long and loud. “When are you going to have guts enough to risk everything you’ve got on yourself—your dreams and goals? When are you going to roll the dice and bet it all on you?”

Complete truth is ALL in my face now. My first want was to put her in her place. I wanted to say, “I am your mother and you cannot talk to me like that!” But for what ever reason, nothing came out, I could not say a word and her words marinated to my core. Within minutes, it was as if somebody opened the floodgates of my wounded soul and uncontrollable tears just came rushing out. After managing to pull the car off to the side of the highway, I just set there and had me a good ole fashioned gut-wrenching, cry.

That night, those truths, were the beginning of a very uncomfortably tough reconditioning regiment of my mind and spirit. A reconditioning that needed my total consent and willingness to invest in me, to roll the dice and bet it all on Pennie. To shut out the internal and external naysayer, to hush the voice of criticism and complaint. And to fight a personal fight of reconciliation and forgiveness. To give myself permission to be the student, instead of the teacher, the one in need of healing, instead of being the fixer. To nurture others to a state of self-sufficiency, instead of being the enabler or rescuer. To accept a time of receiving, without the guilt or perceive obligation to give in return. To know that it does not all depend on me and I do not have to know everything. To simply bask in the glory and splendor of finally being ME.

Investing in ourselves will take devotion, time and money. Which means we will have to make a conscious commitment and effort to take the time to relax, meditate or just do nothing and know that our personal worth is not diminished, the world will not come crumbling down around us because we allow others to problem-solve for themselves instead of rescuing them.

We have to have the willingness to invest some real money on being around the people or in the environments that will encourage us to acknowledge, own and strengthening our definable skills. Instead of spending money on the latest fashion trend or the hottest video game box for the kids, invest in books (avoid romance novels), tapes, seminars and classes that stretch, enrich, defy, challenge and strengthen our substance.

Motivational speaker Les Brown once told me that my personal growth library should have a value of 10% of my clothing wardrobe. Like me then, some of us have some investing to do. I have also learned that at least 5% of every 24-hour day should be dedicated to enhancing and developing our attitude, character and skills.

Remember, our tapestry of success is self-styled, rich with a combination of many intricate parts and these parts are difficult to follow or analyze by anyone other than its creator.

"He has achieved success who has lived well, laughed often and loved much; who has enjoyed the trust of pure women, the respect of intelligent men and the love of little children; who has filled his niche and accomplished his task; who has left the world better than he found it, whether by an improved poppy, a perfect poem, or a rescued soul; who has never lacked appreciation of Earth's beauty or failed to express it; who has always looked for the best in others and given them the best he had; whose life was an inspiration; whose memory a benediction."

—*Betty Anderson Stanley*

Permissive Power Challenge

Throughout the day, whenever you think of it, challenge yourself to have 5% more faith and trust in your skills, gifts and talents.

Again, it is not your task to be concerned with what your skills, gifts and talents are. Even if you have identified what your skills and talents are, with all diligence resist the temptation to package, compare and dictate their course this only limits their greater potential of being.

In addition, I challenge you to permit yourself to use 5% of your 24-hour day (that's 1 hour and 20 minutes) totally on you and this does not include sleeping.

Your only task here is to gain 5% more faith and trust in your skills, gifts or talents and to use 5% of your day on you. If you permit yourself to experience the simplicity of this, your genuine skills, gifts and talent will begin to surface in more defined and expressive ways then ever imagined.

Remember: There is no time span as to how long to challenge you and there are no pre-determined results or events.

5

What's the Shortest Distance?

"From now on you will be traveling the road between who you think you are and who you can be. The key is to allow yourself to make the journey."
—Disney's "The Princess Diaries"

Through out this book I have said it is not my intent to change minds, but to challenge the comfort of our present mind-set. To allow the mind to do what it does best—think, reason and apply knowledge. However, if after reading this book we do nothing different, then it would be reasonable to belief one of several things. We have not had enough of the dumb stuff yet. Or before we begin the process of self-permission, we need to first develop and strengthen our abilities of self-trust, self-confidence and self-knowledge. And maybe perhaps helplessness is our way of getting the attention we want but feel we might not receive if we were self-possessing and strong.

No matter what reason we conjure up for remaining stuck, the truth is that life will only allow us the privilege of living in denial for so long. More importantly, our spirit will not be denied its purpose to manifest the glory of God. Yes, giving ourselves permission is about change, and for most, the very suggestion of change is a frightening thought. However, the change that self-permission will cause is <u>not</u> as drastic, <u>not</u> as devastating as our imagination will exaggerate it to be.

Let me be perfectly honest. While on our path, there will be days that seem as if we are in an all-out war between the old self wanting to remain intact and the new self waiting to emerge. On other days, it will require a little effort to stay committed, focused and in good spirits, and others will be kickback days of "I can do this!" But if we can remain tenacious and strong fibered on those days of doubt and discomfort, I assure you the success that awaits us is incomprehensible.

June Jordan, poet and civil rights activist, said, "Self-determination has to mean that the leader is your individual gut, heart and mind. Who's really going to care whether you live or die, and who's really going to know the most intimate motivation for your laughter and your tears? You—and you are the only person to be trusted to speak for you and to decide what you will or will not do."[15]

The Real Gift Is In the Going

In Chapter 4, I shared with you my conversation with God concerning my thoughts of His partiality. I have since learned that self-perception is everything. The only difference between a winner and a loser, the successful and the unsuccessful, the weak and the strong is the thoughts, attitudes and perceptions they have of themselves. It has nothing to do with who they know, their ability, or skills—it has everything to do with their internal thoughts and beliefs of themselves and their abilities.

It would be naïve of me to believe that everyone wants the freedom, liberty, independence and authority that self-permission gives. Contrary to belief, with this kind of autonomy comes the obligation of responsibility, and because of this, many will teeter-totter on whether to truly commit to the act of self-permissiveness.

As a society of highly educated, financially savvy, well-intended people, we have somehow begun to see being responsible as archaic and troublesome. We embrace, tolerate and in some cases even encourage the indulgence of every whimsical idea and act. Yet, at the same time, we are also encouraging a mind-set that disregards accountability for the consequences of those indulgences. In essence, we want to have it all, with no responsibility at all. We may want to be self-governing, but we don't want the responsibility of doing the work and maintaining the character.

Let me give you an example of what I mean. I remember hearing a radio commercial that promised complete restoration of phone service. No problem, but then the announcer says, "and that's not even the good part—you don't even have to pay your old phone bill off," then another voice says excitedly, "All right! Cause I owe a bundle!" Excuse me if I am missing the big picture, but isn't this creating a mind-set that disregards and snubs responsibility?

Another example—while finalizing the particulars of a workshop with a group of public school teachers and counselors on rebuilding their morale and dedication, I learned of an incentive program that blew me away. In an effort to get students to do what would benefit them in life—stay in school and learn—this incentive program pays a salary to those who are failing because of poor attendance. Where is the wisdom in this? What are we creating in the minds of our future leaders, parents and decision makers?

Now, I mention this because it is said that "the shortest distance between two points is a straight line." Moving from the subordinate position to the owner and authority of our life's choices will be a process, a journey that will require time, discipline and most importantly, responsibility. The *power of self-permission* demands an increased ability to be self-managed; otherwise, there is the risk of perverting what was to be right and good. Two of the strongest qualities of being self-managed are the ability to delay gratification and the ability to be accountable for our decisions and actions.

About now you are probably saying, 'Hold up, stop the press, I brought this book expecting to learn the *simplest* path to successful living, but all I have read requires real effort on my part.' You're right, so let me explain the sanity behind this perceived madness.

An old adage says, "Many would rather go a long distance out of the way than to go a short distance the right way." Yes, many of us would rather do anything to avoid the possible pain and discomfort of dealing with the real—or right things. We are creatures of comfort, and we will fight to an unusual extent to sustain that comfort. To believe that we would purposely expose ourselves to the excruciating pain of inner truths and self-knowing is insane. Sadly, while we emphatically refuse the pains of knowing our deeper self, we often expose ourselves to the many ruinous people, situations and environments in our lives—that are just as painful—all in the name of love, recognition and belongingness.

There are no quick fixes, no instant mixes when we are seeking to reclaim or to develop our self-permissive power. Hear me. There are absolutely none, and anyone who tries to sell you on that is not about moving people to permanent personal success. It is my absolute, strongest belief that quick fixes merely offer to people what I refer to as *revolving door* remedies—temporary fixes that result in repeated visits to acquire another fix. Now, how much time, effort and pain are we eliminating when we have to deal with the same recurring, self-defeating issues and dilemmas again and again. The irony is, each time the issue, situation, or circumstance returns, it returns with a greater vengeance and a deeper hold—all the while building immunity against our quick-fix efforts.

Remember, I said earlier that 'how to' methods are a one-size fits all approach, which is a setup for failure. They give the optical illusion that all is well, while the cancerous issues continue to fester. Picture this: We are moving along in life, happy about our effortless progress, completely unaware of the assassin within who has been plotting, crouching in hiding—then BAM! Just when things couldn't get any worst, those damnable negative behaviors, attitudes and issues make a surprise attack, causing mass destruction and terror on our mental and emotional confidence. Why did this happen? Simple, we went for instant, quick gratification, instead of doing our real self-work.

When the glitter of the quick or instant falls short of the promises—and they always do—we are likely to experience emotional ebbs. Ultimately, we lose ground and time recovering from the setback and disappointment. The immediate, instant or quick is the enemy of complete and true change and wellness. While the 'how to's' appear to be the simplest path, in the end they actually cause us to exert greater amounts of time, resources and energy. Therefore, while the quick and effortless methods are cute and very enticing, my advice is to *run fast*, *avoid diligently* and *curse profusely* their alluring temptations.

My grandmother would always tell me when I wanted to rush through a process to get to the result, "If you don't have time to do it right the first time, what makes you think you will have time to do it a second time?" Hence, the shortest, simplest path to any destination is the straight and direct approach. The straight and direct path will call for a series of collective actions, and changes and then dealing with the fallout of those changes. It is a continuous effort that will move us in a chosen direction without curving, deviating, embellishing or modifying our course. The greatest gift of going the straight direct path—it never allows us to run from experiencing our authentic reality.

When I say the real gift is in the going, it is because of the fullness I *now* experience because I stayed the course. When I decided with real passion to continue and not turn back, accepting the humiliation, awkwardness and my perceived brokenness as lessons, God leveled the field to assure my success. Unbeknownst to me, God had been maneuvering me around the ditches and minefields all along—and some of those ditches were of my masterful doing. There is a very, very large sign that hangs from a building not far from my office that says, "Please, protect me from what I want!" Obviously, the proprietors know the stresses that follow the ditches we dig ourselves.

As the process of regaining our self-permissive power begins, we will face many challenges, but remember this is just the stage of "Flushing-Out" (Chapter 3). Many days will feel utterly confusing, but nonetheless, don't throw in the towel. We must realize that God promises, "whether we turn right or left, there is a voice behind us saying, this is the way—walk *therein*." The word "therein" signifies having instructions to move in this place, at this time, on this thing or situation. Therefore, we must stay awake to these instructions. I say this because as humans, at the first sign of pain we want to black it out by ways as subtle as overeating or overt as drugs—we need to stop that. Once we gain the courage to wake up, we need to stay awake.

Leveling the Field

In Hosea, God reprimands the people by saying, "My people are destroyed for a lack of knowledge and many have even rejected knowledge."[16] It is my strong opinion that this is still a present day dilemma. English novelist George Eliot reflects, "Knowledge is power. But it is a power reined by scruple, having a conscience of what must be and what may be. Whereas ignorance is a blind giant who, let him but wax unbound, would make it a sport to seize the pillars that hold up the long-wrought fabric of human good and turn all the places of joy as dark as a buried Babylon."[17]

My intent here is a precautionary measure that will level the field and act as a shield to safeguard against possible failure. Only upfront knowledge and foresight will give us this necessary advantage. Although God promises us guidance in our emotional and mental blindness, there is no need to embrace ignorance when we can avoid it. They say "*mistake*" is a label we put on our behavior at a time when our awareness has changed. If you're like me, when I finally decided to wake up I quickly realized how much time I had already forfeited. My request became: God, help me to see what I am doing so I can save myself some time, pain and effort.

See, I have learned when we are fully aware of the consequences of the choices we make and are still willing to pay the cost, we experience fewer reasons to label our choices "mistakes." Although we may experience frustration with the outcome, we will still see it as an opportunity for learning and as exposure to growth. Therefore, we strengthen and develop trust and confidence in our ability to make decisions. If, on the other hand, we have limited awareness of the possible consequences and then are unwilling to pay the price at the time due—the internal affects are defeatism, blame and, over time, injury to our self-trust. This also sets the stage for seeking permission from others, instead of trusting ourselves.

In choosing to regain our self-permissive power, we will face a very worthy opponent, one that is skilled and masterful at keeping us enslaved. In Chapter 1, I used the analogy of Luke Skywalker's battle from Star Wars to describe this internal combat. Before entering the cave, Master Yoda warned him of the fate that would await him if he were unsuccessful. He admonished him to be on guard, for if he, Skywalker, failed at this last and most important challenge, all other subsequent challenges would be lost to him. Although a muppet character, Yoda's words are complete and total truth. If we fail to govern the compulsive opponent within, all of our endeavors are subject to its control.

If we are to be strong, successful winners, there must be an act of abandoning what we have always done. We must declare a leaving of what is familiar, taking a risk, possibly even winding up in a state of temporary isolation for the sake of our newness. How, why or when we step out beyond our familiar is of no great concern. What should be our primary concern is that we be willing to leave behind a portion of our identity in order to become a separate, individuated person. In our stepping out toward success, we must remember that en route there will be a gap between who we were and who we will be. It is in this gap that true self-commitment and self-determination will reign supreme.

En route, we will experience the grief, regret and guilt of leaving behind friends and loved ones. The aloneness, in the beginning, will cause our sad stories of pain, betrayal and abuse to surface, and we may detour in hopes of finding a rest area. Temporary time-outs in my opinion are necessary, but make sure they are in fact temporary and beware the Woolgatherers, Nay Sayers and Red Herrings.

The Woolgatherers are people who consume our time with fanciful stories of how great they could have been if only… or how awesome they *used* to be. The Red Herrings are those who engage us in pointless conversations and gimmicks in order to cloud or confuse our focus. And of course, the Nay Sayers are those people who have more than enough horror stories of their futile travels. They say their warnings of disaster are out of concern for our well-being; actually, they are aimed at paralyzing us so we too can become stuck in pain and bitterness, as they are.

We have all experienced a time when we kept telling a particular sad story repeatedly—perhaps for years. Then one day we're telling our sad story and we realize we're exhausted, and then we think, "How long have I been telling this story, and how many people are as exhausted as I am of hearing it?" I recall once hearing a speaker say, that of the people we tell our sad stories to, 80% don't care and the other 20% are glad it's you and not them.

On the real path, anyone we may meet are "like-travelers" and will only be mildly impressed because his or her stories are the same, if not worse. "Like-travelers" know the value of preserving emotional energy, so we are not inclined to entertain the extended version of a "*somebody done me wrong song,*" and complaining is rarely accepted. Therefore, there will be no fanfare, special treatment or attention given because we chose to take the journey. Keep in mind, this is not for the applause and or the sympathy of others—it is for our finishing, for the restoring of our self-honor, self-dignity and self-trust.

Psychologist Erich Fromm said, "Man's main task in life is to give birth to himself, to become what he potentially is. The most important product of his effort is his own personality."[18] The power of self-permissiveness is not to be taken lightly. If the task of self-permissiveness were so easy, many would have done it by now. Personally, I know I would have, but I found that easy was not an option. Denying, ignoring, pretending, trying to hide and the list of others things we use to make it easy are just useless attempts to avoid facing the real reasons for our behaviors. Again, expecting the reclaiming of self to pose no difficulties is equivalent to insisting that fool's gold is real.

Let me say this from my heart: Do not, repeat, <u>do</u> <u>not</u>, initiate stepping out for any other reason but your own. If we are not prepared mentally and emotionally to make the trek to higher ground, we are sure to experience further injury. Remember that how, why or when we step out is of no great concern. Forcing ourselves to take action at the urging of another when we have no conviction is the same as self-inflicted injury. This will only lead to bitterness and resentment toward ourselves and the other person. One thing that we can be assured of—that if we are taking too long to commit to our betterment, life will happen to us and we will have to go—or die. So, I would sincerely rather you wait until you are completely ready than to start and turn back. Starting and stopping will only intensify our fears and hesitations, which will slow or prevent any future progress or movement.

Up to this point in my life, I know the effort and self-loyalty required for regaining self-permission, so I refuse to give a bunch of rah-rah without truth. So in the spirit of the ones before me, it is my intent to share some wisdom that will assist you in assuring success.

The three areas in which we will need to watch, in order to gain the advantage on our path, are *self-induced resistance*, *taking giant steps* and *attempting a quick comeback*. I will address each of these areas later in the chapter, but first I want to share an experience of professional development that will set up their explanation nicely. As the story unfolds, although it has professional references, look for the similarities that apply to our commitment and responsibility for regaining our power of self-permission.

Not too long ago, two friends and I attended a professional development weekend for entrepreneurs who seriously wanted to grow their businesses. This three-day weekend, called the Achiever's Circle, held in La Jolla, California, was a place I had never heard of—and I have relatives who live in California. Two months before attending this workshop, I received a four-page preplanning questionnaire. A month later, I received confirmation of my acceptance and an attendee packet, which included the weekend's agenda and other essential information.

After reading over all the material, a few statements stood out as glaring challenges for me to assess my intent and expectations for attending. The first statement said, "If you are willing to roll up your sleeves and assume the predominant responsibility for your success, you can expect results." The second said, "We are looking for Doers and Achievers only. Thinkers and Strugglers need not apply. This program is not designed for people in transition or trying to discover their life's purpose. This experience is for people who want to make something happen in their lives now, not some time down the road." And the third statement said, "Don't make a commitment you cannot keep. Once notified of your acceptance, you show up.

Looking at the packet I now held in my hands was proof that I had been accepted for the program, so there was no backing out. Looking over those three statements again, I thought, "Snap! What the heck have I done to myself now—and where in hell is this La Jolla?"

Coming from three different states, my friends and I meet up a day before the program was to begin. Though we came excited, we also came bearing our own expectations, anxieties and hopes. La Jolla turned out not to be a remote place in hell, but a beautiful village community in San Diego, right off the coast of the Pacific Ocean.

On the morning of the class, we were given the day's agenda along with other materials and more rules consisting of confidentiality, timeliness and an admonishment to use the weekend as a time of introspection, not socialization. After introducing himself, our host and instructor Mark LeBlanc, looked at us and with solid confidence and ease said, "It is not my intent to entertain you for the weekend, but to put a jetpack on your butts to move you beyond your present thoughts of your potential." The weekend turned out to be more than the eight of us in attendance expected.

Now, just in case the life similarities were missed let me put in the way it came glaring at me:

"*Your life's success is your predominant responsibility. If you want to remain a Thinker or a Struggler, don't bother, because this achiever's path is for people who want to make something happen now. So if you show up—show up totally, mind, body and emotions otherwise don't make a commitment you cannot keep.*"

The Path of Least Resistance

I would love to tell you that life is a little bit nicer when dealing with our development, but I can't, because it's not. There are forces in our lives whose main function is to test our commitment and loyalty, to demand that we obligate ourselves to our growth. If we are unaware of this fact and the intent of these forces, we will mistakenly label them as difficult people or situations, or even worse, as punishment. Misunderstanding this will move us back to the mind of a struggler and in our attempt to resist or fight back, we become stuck, distracted and off course. This is not a dilemma known only to the struggler. We run the risk of these hindrances at any and every level of advancement, no matter who we are.

Of what I can share about my weekend in La Jolla, the three of us, although friends, went with different experiences and definitions of what we considered success. Those different definitions and experiences had different needs and expectations, and the three of us had a face-off with our predominant sabotaging behaviors and thoughts that had brought us there. Believing the successful or talented never deal with lost focus and mind freezes is unrealistic. In fact, there are many people with outstanding potential and talent, yet they lack clarity, direction and discipline.

Our path can be one with the least possible amounts of stress, pressure and apprehension, if we are mindful of *self-induced resistance*, *taking giant steps* and *attempting a quick comeback.* Ironically, to my knowledge, of the eight in attendance that weekend, three of us, including myself, found out that we were dealing with one of these areas as a hindrance to our success. We boarded planes returning to our perspective paths of success armed with a phrase of insight that spoke directly to our hindrance, which I will share.

Self-Induced Resistance

Giving ourselves permission begins first with the decision to change. Once we decide to change, we must also decide to do what ever it will take to make that change. However, many of us never really *decide,* at least not with conviction. We threaten to change. We promise to change if conditions don't get rough. We change under duress. We even use change as a tool to manipulate others.

Our self-induced resistance is clever and can come in many forms. The subtler, more elusive and more non-offensive it appears, the more skilled and deeply ingrained it is. Self-induced resistance is beguiling, because it appears to be helpful, but it is the enemy of movement and is more injurious and harmful than external resistance. I understand how shrewd and ingenious self-induced resistance is, and that's the reason I suggest introducing new information and behavior to our psyche in 5% doses. Introducing change of any kind in larger doses at the onset will only cause our old psyche to perceive it as mutiny and will rebel as a form of retribution.

One participant of the group found out that weekend how easy it is to fall into the subtle allure of self-induced resistance disguised as opportunity. Convinced that all of her non-connecting projects and great ideas would eventually come together and lead to success, she worked fervently on all of them. Flip-flopping from one great idea to another caused her the frustrations of feeling scattered, with no real direction or plan. Because she stayed so busy, usually overwhelmed by her ineffectual efforts, she was unable to see that her real path lay in her heart's desire.

She admitted to getting many glaring confirmations to what she was to do, but resisted giving into her inner wisdom. She often brushed it off as an area of interest no one really cared about—convinced that the other projects held a greater value to society. The busywork also prevented moments of stillness that would have revealed the true resistance was her fears of feeling inadequate. Even though she holds a doctor's degree in the area of her true interest, she cringed at the thought of being judged and found deficient. This is a common fear of those of us who suffer with perfectionism. Her phrase of insight: "With no plan in place, it is easy to go off on tangents disguised as opportunities. There is power in a written plan."[19]

Changing our external patterns of behavior is usually *just the tip of the iceberg* and is often insufficient. This is why we have such a high rate of recidivism and emotional underdevelopment within our society—we go for superficial results. Our self-sabotaging and self-destructive behaviors are the results of the irreconcilable difference we have internally, and many of these difference have nothing to do with other people. Greek philosopher Aristotle said, "We are what we repeatedly do. Excellence, then, cannot be an act, but must be a habit." Since all action originates in our thoughts—if deep infinite change is to take place—then the ultimate habit to disassemble is our thought habits of self-deprecation. We can only accomplish this by devoting reasonable time and effort to periods of aloneness for personal evaluation and planning.

Our resistant self will mask self-deprecation or undervaluing our abilities as modesty or humbleness. When in fact, it is the internal foe that hides our light and causes self-distrust, timidity. When we do not learn to regard, consider and respect ourselves, by ourselves, we will fall back into old habits and wait for someone else to validate us in order to be consoled and to feel safe during our moments of weakness.

To accomplish this under the least amount of resistance we have to be alert to our every word, act and thought. At the slightest inclination or prelude of self-negativity, *stop*, *recognize* and *remodel*! Stop the act or thought in that very moment—not the next time, but this time. Recognize the negative impact it has had up to this point. Then remodel that thought or act—not after someone else, but after your intended sufficient self. Ah, ah, ah—our intended self is not based on anyone else's past opinions or expectations, not even our own. It is solely based on truth, and our God conscious knows exactly who we where intended to be. All we have to do is give ourselves permission to experience and *be* that person, to embrace that good thought, or feel that good feeling.

Will this remodeling happen immediately? No—thank God. Along with knowing who we were intended to be, our internal truth also knows what, when and how much we can take in order to rebuild correctly. As an ex-police officer, I spent many years working with shelters for battered women. It wasn't until I had my own experience with abuse that I learned that my previous work with the shelters was merely superficial. I came to understand the strong emotional grip a toxic relationship has on both victim and violator. Because of this emotional grip, the abused will return to their abuser an average of seven times before making a successful, permanent break.

Self-induced resistance holds the same damnable grip. Therefore, as I said before, once we decide to change, we must also decide to do whatever it will take to make that change, and as many times as it will take. One substantiating factor most quick fix remedies leave out is there is no such thing as overnight success. Success worth having takes time and effort. Mark Twain said it best, "Habit is habit and not to be flung out of the window by any man, but coaxed downstairs a step at a time."[20]

Taking Giant Steps

People often accuse me of being analytical, and as you would suspect, I totally deny that accusation. Because actually, I am metaphorical and a storyteller by nature, and as you might have gather by now, I also love quotes. I figure that if eloquently said once, why say it again. But I digressed.
Anyway, one of my all time favorite movies is “Contact,” staring actress extraordinaire Jodi Foster. It is a movie about staying the course in the face of great loss, defeat, lack of support, lack of recognition, betrayal—and a band of people who flat-out think you’re a crazed, obsessed loon. Every movie that makes my best movie list, whether cartoon, drama, romance, etc., has a classic line that speaks to my spirit. The classic line for me in this movie came twice when Jodie Foster’s character was told by her father in a moment of elation over a new-found skill, “Small steps, Ellie—small steps.”

Taking giant steps, wanting to run, not walk, is the most common error after an awakening. When we finally realize just how much time, opportunity and advantage has actually passed us by, our eagerness to make up for the lost time causes us to act in frantic haste. There are times when we must seize opportunity expeditiously, but misdirected haste is the greatest waste of time and effort known to man or woman.

This is where I tell on myself. On the first day of instruction in La Jolla, we were to write down a dollar amount of what our expected optimistic monthly income would be. This amount was to be based solely on our present-day profit centers and would be known as our optimistic number. We all wrote down our dollar amount and later shared it openly with the group. After a long moment of silence, the instructor looked at us and said, “Of all the groups I have worked with, these are the highest numbers ever.” Having the third highest number in the group, I proudly reclined back in my chair. After an hour of information, our instructor asked if anyone wanted to change his or her optimistic number—we all declined. Before ending the first day, we received our assignment for the evening and were told to look at our optimistic number again just in case we would like to change it the next day.

I found myself agitated by his insistence of changing our numbers, as if he wanted us to question or doubt ourselves. He said his intent was to move us beyond our present possibilities, so why was he now challenging that possibility? The more I thought about it, the more I was convinced he was trying to minimize our ambitions. Throughout the evening, my gentle inner voice would say, "Pennie, your number is too high, you're not being fair to yourself. It's about sure steps now, no need to run—you're going to get there." My agitation being much louder than my voice of wisdom, I chose to dismiss my wisdom as a traitor, falling for the scare tactic of an intellectual bully. In my head, I created a scenario that reeked of hidden sabotage and restrain. By bedtime, his insistence had become a personal insult.

The next morning I sat in class suspicious and even more determined to stick with my number, waiting for the opportunity to question his motives. As expected, he asked if anyone want to reconsider his or her number. We all sat silent. After a few minutes he slowly rose from his chair, looked at us and gave what became my phrase of insight: "This group has high conviction, but low commitment." After making that statement he turned and began writing something on the board. Not one word was passed among the entire group.

That one phrase, probably passing over everyone else in the room, cut me like a knife. Finishing what he was doing on the board, he turned to explain how each one of us had set optimistically high goals. He went on to say while those numbers might make us feel good, they would also be the quickest and surest way to fail. Using the template drawn on the board, he took our present profit centers and our numbers and began to show us how stressful and draining it would be to obtain such goals. In essence, we would no longer love the work we did, but what we loved would be working us—and that's not success. His insistence was not to minimize our ambitions, but the motive of a sage to his students to judge wisely.

Having a major in low self-regard and a minor in people-pleasing and perfectionism, I was forever setting myself up with such unreasonable goals and decisions. In my hotel room that night, I faced acknowledging several things. First, my agitation with his insistence to change the number symbolized the bitter taste I still had for the many times I had been told, "You're a peon and no matter what you do, you'll always be a peon." Secondly, every past gigantic step, goal and decision, had been made with one purpose in mind—to prove that I was more than a peon.

You see, up until that moment I believed that exceptional people took exceptionally giant steps. If I was ever to erase the shameful identity of a peon, I too had to take giant steps. In that moment, I realized that an exceptional step does not mean taking steps beyond our balance. Exceptional really means being the best that we are capable of being at that time, in that situation. Exceptional demands from us nothing outside of our capacity of being or performing.

I also realized I had forgotten that I had given myself permission to reconcile with my past. Forgetting this, led me to a momentary act of regression. That regression caused me to misinterpret the instructor's intent, which escalated to inward expressions of misguided discontentment. However, the most damnable thing that I did was to choose to disregard my inner wisdom, dismissing it as having abandoned me for the other side.

The real secret to staying on the simplest path to success is to know that having it all does not mean having it all at once. This means embracing the act of taking smaller, well balanced steps, so we can accomplish our goals with the least amount of resistance. Keep in mind that taking giant steps after "recovery" of any kind is a sign of an amateur. Other common errors linked to taking giant steps are:

Feelings of guilt or self-reproach because we are no longer acting in haste. When our acts become more deliberate and intentional, we appear to be progressing leisurely. To a mind that is high-strung or accustomed to operating in the crisis mode, *leisure* communicates a state of sloth, irresponsibility or a lack of motivation.

We set goals based on what we think we "should" be doing. The *woulda*, *shoulda*, *coulda's* of life can be exhausting, especially when they are constantly haunting us internally. In an attempt to quiet the voices of "at this age, I should be able to…" "With the education I have I could've…" and "if I were you, I would've…" we take steps based on unrealistic expectations, rather than on what we can actually do at that moment, with what we have. We have a tendency to beat ourselves up with the remark, "If I only knew then what I know now." Well, take a breather. The only reason we know now is because of what we went through then. The *woulda, shoulda, coulda's* can also cause us to be unwilling to delay gratification, be overly eager, even desperate and greedy, which leads to taking giant steps.

We fail to acknowledge and honor our fears. Often, in an attempt to prove something, as an act of defiance or revenge, we may disregard strong feelings of hesitation, apprehension or mistrust. Failing to at least acknowledge and consider our fears and discomforts will cause us to fall flat on our face or become paralyzed and do nothing. Don't mistake acknowledging and honoring our feelings of mistrust or apprehension as a justification of inactivity. Sometimes our fears are simply growing pains, or an indication that we are taking too big a step. Slowing down to embrace ourselves or resolving to take baby steps will relieve the stress and anxieties. It will also allow us to hear and understand what our fears are really saying.

What our instructor embedded that weekend, at least in my mind was, we may have great ambition—an eager or strong desire to achieve something. We may even have high conviction—a fixed or strong belief. However, if we are unrealistic, taking giant steps to achieve, instead of balanced steps to succeed, we will have low commitment—and we will not have the emotional and intellectual bound needed to stay the course.

Attempting a Quick Comeback

"Caution has its place, no doubt, but we cannot refuse our support to a serious venture which challenges the whole of the personality. If we oppose it, we are trying to suppress what is best in man—his daring and his aspirations. And should we succeed, we should only have stood in the way of that invaluable experience which might have given a meaning to life. What would have happened if Paul had allowed himself to be talked out of his journey to Damascus?"[21]

—Carl Jung

Giving ourselves permission will awaken more than just our present conscience. At the very decision of accepting *predominant responsibility* for our life's success, there will be a second birthing, a resurrecting of issues, thoughts, behaviors and feelings that we previously considered dead. It is the reality of possibly resurrecting these hurts, losses and pains that are the incentive to believing they are better left dead. While we might do a good job at anesthetizing our 10% conscious self through external placebos, our 60% heart and body knows (Chapter 3). Remember, the greatest gift of going the straight and direct path is that it never allows us to run from experiencing our authentic reality. Hence, we never have to deal with the recurring residue of our past later.

We have all heard the phrases, "Let sleeping dog lie," "Let the past stay in the past," "Let bygones be bygones" or "Why dig up dead issues?" Many, after making the commitment to regain their power of self-permission, will start their trek believing they can simply leave reality behind. Not so. Every past reality, if not dealt with, will become our present and future companion. We can publicly deny our upsets and even talk ourselves out of acknowledging the emotional impact of a major loss, but our 60% soul knows the real deal. From the book "I Could Do Anything, If I Only Knew What It Was," Barbara Sher with Barbara Smith note, "You can't put something down until you've picked it up. You can't put tears behind you until you've wept them. You can't let go of the past until you've grieved for it."

For those of us who are leaders, perfectionist, known by our tough veneer, the highly spiritual and the "I'm too old for that" crowd, this will be a major feat. However, let me assure you of a very real truth: Unreconciled secrets and hurts devastate—even kill our very breath of life. Fast-forwarding through our internal injuries will stunt proper growth and recovery.

I remember a friend sharing his experience of a broken limb from a football game that had improperly healed. He said the doctor advised him that if he wanted to regain the full use of his limb he would have to allow the limb to be purposely broken again in order to reset it properly. Of course he agreed, but he said if he had known how much more painful the second break would have been, he would have refused the procedure. This analogy signifies the very reason we attempt a quick comeback—to avoid the pain of a secondary break. The thought of letting our hearts break all over again is frightful to even the best of us. We think that if we surrender to the sorrows we feel, it would literally wipe us out.

As mentioned in Chapter 3, revisiting the memory of what was snatched from us before we were completely ready to release it can be extremely painful. And attempting a quick comeback is our way of leapfrogging past the conscious awareness of these irrevocable losses and the residue of our neurotic choices that stemmed from our insecurities, anxieties, depression and irrational fears. However, failing to truly reconcile with those hurts, especially if we feel at fault for the loss, will only act as a resistant to our success. We will never be able to see the full extent of our possibilities, know the fullness of joy that is our promise as humans or comprehend our worthiness of a greater future, without first allowing our hurts and pains to run their course.

On the night before our class was to end in La Jolla, our instructor hosted a group dinner party. After all we had been through, it was great to have a relaxing evening of great food and stimulating conversation with new "like-travelers." When the evening had ended, another participant and I found ourselves walking in the same direction to our hotels. As we walked along the serene but busy streets of this beautiful community, we continued one of the pervious dinner conversations. We found ourselves sitting on a bench watching people walking along engaged in quiet conversations, as we were.

In class, my companion had appeared to be well balanced in thought and direction. My internal question as he interacted in the class was, "Why is he here?" As we shared our pleasure in being a part of this experience, the conversation took an unexpected turn. His voice, now coming from his authentic self, began to reveal his purpose for being there. He spoke of a time past when he first stared opportunity in the face. Being so sure, he threw caution out the window and jumped in headfirst. Like a ram, he charged through, avoiding all the yield signs and barely pausing for the stop signs of life. As his story began to climax, his tempo slowed and he confessed that while throwing out caution, he somehow managed to throw out a few other very important things as well. As fate would have it, the collision course he had set in place happened.

With the loss of everything he valued and more, his resolve was to "carry on, don't look back." Ignoring and denying were his weapons of choice. That seemed to be the best remedy, because within two short years life had given him a second chance. He went on to say that he had been living by the declaration, "You can't keep a good man down, because he'll come back bigger and better than before."

For the last year, he had been working full throttle to accomplish his great comeback. Yet he felt as if he was at a great impasse, unable to move. He confessed that he came to La Jolla expecting to get a greater sense of direction and even more fuel. Instead he had experienced a surprise attack from his past. The impasse was not the problematic people and circumstances he had been blaming, but his own hidden fears of rejection, failure and loss. This residue resulted from his past wounds, wounds he had so neatly dismissed years before.

Ending his conversation, he noticed the time that had passed. I realized I had not said a word—I am usually never without words. As we walked to our hotels, there was no further talk of what had just taken place. As if to pick up right where we left off before, we spoke of the night air, the beauty of the moon reflecting on the ocean. In parting, he paused for a moment and said with a slight smile, "You know what I learned today? I learned that if you put together the right model for not just your business, but your life, you will have a greater chance of your fun meter being on maximum and your stress meter being on minimum."[22] That was his phrase of insight.

As he permitted himself to be transparent through conversation, there were three thoughts that rested in my mind: Although achievers are long distance runners, they <u>don't</u> move at top speed for the duration of the race, so they have had to learn a few things:

Achievers learn how to pace themselves. Sagely, achievers don't try to make every area of their life a top priority at the same time. By knowing and respecting our limitations, we can eliminate the stresses that come from overextending ourselves. And once we understand our life's rhythm, we will then begin to develop and implement according to those stages.

Achievers prioritize their lives. By simply taking a moment to weigh the importance of one life's goal in relation to another (without the manipulation of internal or external guilt), we can establish a balanced plan that is rewarding to both our personal and professional pursuits.

Most importantly, ***achievers know the significance of focusing on one life area, while nurturing the others.*** Learning to focus on our own top priorities and not the priorities and demands of others will be tough. After spending a large portion of our lives putting the desires of others above our own, learning not to be a superhero will be quite challenging for many of us. But the power of self-permission requires the releasing of others in our lives to do what they are capable of—standing on their own. By encouraging self-sufficiency within others, we stand a greater chance of gaining assistance from them later, and having more time to dedicate to ourselves.

As we parted company that night he said, "I wonder if my so-called big comeback would have really impressed anyone. But that doesn't even matter now. When I get back home, the first thing I am going to do is stop stressing everybody out. Then I'm going to stop trying to prove whatever I have been trying to prove, and then I am going to just start having fun—because I really do love what I do." He thanked me for such a stimulating conversation, said a final good night and whistled as he walked down the street to his hotel.

As I watched him go whistling down the street, I realized I had just encountered a life lesson. Because he gave himself permission to grow, to be reconciled within himself, his mind did what it does best—think, reason and apply the knowledge and he had absolutely no help from me.

As you can see, no matter where we are on our path to success our self-sabotaging behaviors and thoughts can cause us to get stuck or off course at anytime. As we grow, understand and strengthen our power of self-permission it will be essential to remember: Success doesn't happen overnight. The only right way of growing is the way God has predestined for each of us as individuals, and self-adoration is paramount if we are to ever properly love and respect others.
My friends and I went seeking the wisdom and knowledge of achievers. The price for that knowledge and wisdom was an introspective weekend that demanded from us a "put-up or shut-up" mentality. An investment in ourselves that called for leaving our familiar, to discipline ourselves to an imposed structure and to embrace the value of aloneness—even with friends close by. Did we experience bouts of anxiety? Yes! The entire weekend was full of in-your-face internal exposure. Sometimes it even became emotional. There was no pressure to spill our guts about our internal agitations unless we wanted to. And because we were among "like-travelers" we knew that sometimes silence speaks louder, so we respected and honored it.

I always tell people: When we find ourselves experiencing a situation with other people and that situation challenges to stretch and contort us beyond our known abilities, we are in the throes of internal development. Those who are sharing that moment of development are in some way keeping a divine appointment. Maybe their role that day is to agitate, upset and disturb. Maybe their role is to bring the missing piece or to deliver a forgotten message. Whatever their role—our role is to find the common tread of those involved instead of the differences, and watch what kindred spirits do.

The Afterglow

Author and lecturer Helen Keller said, "Knowledge is happiness, because to have knowledge—broad, deep knowledge—is to know true ends from false and lofty things from low. To know the thoughts and deeds that have marked man's progress is to feel the great heartthrobs of humanity through the centuries; and if one does not feel in these pulsations a heavenward striving, one must indeed be deaf to the harmonies of life."[23]

At the age of 15, I found myself an unwed pregnant teenager, living alone, holding a full-time job and struggling to finish high school. Back then, with those kinds of odds against you, many counted you a lost cause. The guilt, shame, ridicule and abandonment had done a good job of lowering my esteem. Managing to finish high school, keep a job, provide shelter, food and clothing for my daughter and to make it to my mid-twenties without getting pregnant again were all great accomplishments. Yet I had failed to shake the grip of my shameful past. While visiting my grandmother one day, she made a statement that would follow me all my life, but it took me 20 more years to implement its truth.

While sharing lunch in her small high-rise apartment, she looked at me and said, "Baby, you are not the first, nor will you be the last young woman who will have a baby out of wedlock. You just need to ask God to forgive you, cause He will—and then get on with living your life." Pausing for a brief moment, she then came back with a finish that is just as potent today as it was then. "The hard part will be believing that He has forgiven you." She gazed into space for a moment then continued with her lunch, never saying any more on that topic. But somehow I knew she was talking from the deepest part of wisdom. It is from this same space that I present these finishing touches.

Self-Forgiveness, the Hardest Part

We hear a lot about the subject of forgiveness these days, at least I do. Radical Forgiveness, The Gift of Forgiveness, Exploring Forgiveness, Forgiveness Is a Choice, No Future Without Forgiveness. Amazon.com, lists 495 book titles on the subject of forgiveness, and Barnes & Noble lists 598 titles. I think it would be fair to say that the subject is well covered, and there is no shortage of available reference material, God knows I have made a sizeable investment in books on the subject myself.

With some 700 books at our disposal, churches on almost every corner, television and radio programs that advocate forgiveness, we are still gridlocked in the area of exercising forgiveness. Families divided, marriages destroyed, communities suffering, violence in the workplace, schools terrorized, nations crippled by the lack of regard for another human life—it's evident that we live in a world occupied by grudge-holders.

There are three things that will motivate people to action or change. Knowledge—the "whats" and "whys" of life. An African Proverb says, "If we know the *whys* in life, we can endure any *how*." Skill—the "how to" of life, or what I like to call knowledge in action. And Desire—the "want to" which is the greatest of all three. When we hold onto unforgiveness, an emotion of bitterness, it is because we *want to*—there is absolutely no other reason, no matter how we try to justify it. As human beings, we are capable of absolute greatness —after the events of September 11th, no one can tell me any different. Many are under the assumption that bitterness and unforgiveness is holding us hostage, when it is we who hold it hostage. If we were to give ourselves permission to open our hands and let go of the grip we have on revenge and bitterness, forgiveness would happen.

There are more than enough reasons for any of us to remain bitter for a lifetime, but how effective would that be? Up to this point, has bitterness and unforgiveness changed our past or elevated our present? Will it make better the fibers of our future? We have the illusion that it is better to be bitter at someone than to turn inward and deal with our pain, disappointment or fear. We also feel that being bitter is a form of fighting back. However, bitterness is actually an emotional expression of severe grief. It indicates the body's need to finish something in order to let it go. Instead of seeing this emotion as an indicator for the need to mourn or lament, we see it as an instrument of control, or as a weapon of war.

The irony in all this is that much of the bitterness and unforgiveness we experience is self-inflicted. We spend a lot of energy cursing the way things are or were in our lives, and we are very unaware of our actions. When we lack the courage to give ourselves permission to grieve our losses, whatever they are, we don't have the capacity to embrace our future. Forgiving our past and present motivates our future. Let me recommend a book that I found most helpful in processing grief: "The Courage To Grieve" by Judy Tatelbaum. The book speaks to the physical loss of a loved one, but I found that by replacing that subject with whatever loss is being experienced, the soul will be quenched and refreshed. Whether it is a job, a house, a relationship or being passed over for a position—loss is loss.

Three years ago when I received my ordination as a minister, I was asked what I would tell a person who struggled with an unforgiving heart. I'm not sure what my response was, but it was incorrect. I have since learned two valuable truths. First, forgiveness doesn't really benefit the other person, it benefits us. It releases us from an emotional prison of pure torment and positions us for the good intended for us. Second, you might as well forgive the other person, because if they acknowledge their wrong and ask God for His grace and forgiveness, He will bestow complete forgiveness—no matter how much anger and contempt we hold for that person.

When I decided to give myself permission to '*let go*' by accepting this truth the first thing I said was, "Dang, I sure hate it," and I walked around for a couple of days with my lip stuck out, because there where some people I really wanted God to zap on my behalf. But I am thankful He protects us from what we want and is patient in the face of our frivolous babble as we grow. And I am most thankful for the deaf ear God has to our poor and unjust opinions of who we are and what we are capable of achieving.

While I speak of our great need of sincere, unconditional forgiveness—no forgiveness is greater than the forgiveness we need so desperately to give to ourselves. From experience let me say this: forgiving others is great and wonderful, but it won't matter until we forgive ourselves. Without the willingness to truly forgive, to reconcile with the "*I*" inside, the "*I*" outside is only going to experience a quarter of the "fullness of joy." I cannot stress enough the important role self-forgiveness plays on our attitude and behavior—no, our lives.

If I were asked what would be my greatest desire for this world, it would be that every person would give himself or herself permission to experience the *embrace* and *love* of self-forgiveness. In doing so, it would allow an outpouring of the same from us to others without suspicion and paranoia. And we would begin to experience the luster life holds in just the simplest of things.

While the journey to regain our *power of self-permission* will be one of effort, discipline, responsibility and commitment, the key to beginning the journey is *passion*—the "want to." I used the word *passion* because it is the most powerful of all human emotions. Passion signifies boundless enthusiasm, and to be enthusiastic is to be in God. The act of giving ourselves permission is much more complex than simply saying it, so it will take the power of passion to complete the task. Keep in mind, that this process cannot be forced, it cannot be rushed. And the most important thing for us to remember while on this path to success is to absorb every lesson in order to share what we will learn with others who may be just beginning.

In closing,

"There can be no knowledge without emotion. We may be aware of a truth, yet until we have felt its force, it is not ours. To the cognition of the brain must be added the experience of the soul."[24]

—Arnold Bennett, British novelist

"And they overcame him by the Blood of the Lamb and the words of their testimonies."

Notes

---

1 Andrea Dworkin (b. 1946), U.S. feminist critic. "The Sexual Politics of Fear and Courage," speech, 12 March 1975, Queens College, City University of New York (published in Our Blood, ch. 5, 1976). (Italics mine)

2 Genesis 12:1-4 The Amplified Bible Zondervan Publishing House

3 Isaiah 42:16 paraphrased from the Life Application Bible New International Version Tyndale House & Zondervan Publication

4 D. H. Lawrence (1885–1930), British author. Shadows.

5 Ronald Reagan (b. 1911), U.S. Republican politician, president. Remark, 13 April 1984, at the annual White House Correspondents' Association dinner.

6 John 4:1-9 22 paraphrased from the Life Application Bible New International Version Tyndale House & Zondervan Publication

7 Proverbs 15:13 & 15 Proverbs 17:22 paraphrased from the Life Application Bible New International Version Tyndale House & Zondervan Publication

8 The American Heritage® Dictionary of the English Language, Third Edition copyright © 1992 by Houghton Mifflin Company.

9 "Forever No More" – poem by Mary J. Blige from her CD "No More Drama" copyright © 2001

10 James 4:2 & 3 paraphrased from the Life Application Bible New International Version Tyndale House & Zondervan Publication

11 Ursula K. Le Guin (b. 1929), U.S. author. "A Left-Handed Commencement Address," to Mills College Class of 1983 (published in: Dancing at the Edge of the World, 1989)

12 Romans 2: 11 paraphrased from the Life Application Bible New International Version Tyndale House & Zondervan Publication

13 André Gide (1869–1951), French author. Journals 1889–1949, "Literature and Ethics" (ed. by Justin O'Brien, 1951), entry in 1901.

14 W. Somerset Maugham (1874–1965), British author. The Summing Up, ch. 48 (1938).

15 June Jordan (b. 1939), U.S. poet, civil rights activist. Moving Towards Home: Political Essays, "Civil Wars" (1989; first published 1981).

16 Hosea 4:6a paraphrased from the Life Application Bible New International Version Tyndale House & Zondervan Publication

17 George Eliot (1819–80), English novelist, editor. Daniel Deronda, bk. 3, ch. 21 (1876).

18 Erich Fromm (1900–1980), U.S. psychologist. Man For Himself, ch. 4 (1947).

19 Mark LeBlanc From his book Growing Your Business. Beaver's Press Edina, MN. 1999

20 Mark Twain (1835–1910), U.S. author. Pudd'nhead Wilson, ch. 6, "Pudd'nhead Wilson's Calendar" (1894).

21 Carl Jung (1875–1961), Swiss psychiatrist. Collected Works, vol. 11, "Psychotherapists or the Clergy" (ed. by William McGuire, 1958).

22 Mark LeBlanc From his book Growing Your Business. Beaver's Press Edina, MN. 1999

23 Helen Keller (1880–1968), U.S. blind/deaf author, lecturer. The Story of My Life, pt. 1, ch. 20 (1903).

24 Arnold Bennett (1867–1931), British novelist. The Journals of Arnold Bennett (1932), entry for 18 March 1897.